Teaching English

Teaching English

Theory and Practice
from Kindergarten to
Grade Twelve

Don Gutteridge

James Lorimer & Company Ltd., Publishers
Toronto, 2000

© 2000 Don Gutteridge

All rights reserved. No part of this book may be reproduced or transmitted in any form or by any means, electronic or mechanical, including photocopying, or by any information storage or retrieval system, without permission in writing from the publisher.

James Lorimer & Company Ltd. acknowledges the support of the Ontario Arts Council. We acknowledge the support of the Government of Canada through the Book Publishing Industry Development Program (BPIDP) for our publishing activities. We acknowledge the support of the Canada Council for the Arts for our publishing program.

Cover: Kevin O'Reilly

Cataloguing in Publication Data

Gutteridge, Don, 1937–
   Teaching English : theory and practice from kindergarten to grade twelve

Includes bibliographical references.
ISBN 1-55028-629-3 (bound)   ISBN 1-55028-627-7 (pbk.)

1. English literature — Study and teaching (Elementary). 2. English literature — Study and teaching (Secondary). I. Title.

LB1575.G877 1999   820.71'2   C99-932847-6

James Lorimer & Company Ltd., Publishers
35 Britain Street
Toronto, Ontario
M5A 1R7

Printed and bound in Canada.

Contents

Introduction		1
1	How We Read	
	The Process of Reading	8
	Reading Poetry	11
2	Aesthetic Reading: Poetry	
	The Thing Itself	20
	Some Pedagogical Principles	34
	Implications for Teaching Poetry	45
	• General Implications	45
	• Kindergarten to Grade Three	49
	• Grades Four to Nine	51
	• Grades Ten to Twelve	58
	Resources	67
3	Aesthetic Reading: Fiction	
	Fiction and Why We Read It	70
	The Process of Reading Fiction	77
	Pedagogical Principles and Implications for Teaching Fiction	83
	A Sample Lesson	90
	Resources	96
4	Poetic Writing	
	Poetic and Expressive	101
	Poetic Writing: Some Practical Suggestions	108
	Resources	113
5	Sound Theory / Good Practice	
	Theory Gone Awry: The Case of Writing Process	115
	The Consequences of Theory	120
Afterword		122
Endnotes		127
Index		145

Acknowledgements

In writing a book that is a kind of summing up after more than thirty years in the business of teaching English, I am acutely aware of how many friends, colleagues and students have contributed — wittingly or otherwise — to my own education. I owe them an immeasurable debt of gratitude, against which this monograph is but token payment. There is not space enough, nor is my memory secure enough, to name them all, but I would be more than remiss if I did not mention four colleagues, among dozens, whose conversation, moral support, and exemplary professionalism have materially affected both the motive and the tenor of my work: Ian Underhill, Geoff Milburn, Colm O'Sullivan and George Martell. To the legions of pupils, students and student teachers who have graced my classrooms over three decades, I can only say a heartfelt thank you.

D.G.
July, 1999

*For the teachers in my family
Anne, John and Kate,
and
for George Martell, educator* extraordinaire

Then felt I like some watcher of the skies
When a new planet swims into his ken;
Or like stout Cortez when with eagle eyes
He stared at the Pacific — and all his men
Looked at each other with a wild surmise,
Silent, upon a peak in Darien.

John Keats
– from "On First Looking into Chapman's Homer"

Introduction

Theory is not a cherished word among teachers, even in the happiest circumstance. And theory about English teaching, where the attainment and development of literacy is paramount, has been no exception. It has proved to be the most contentious area of educational debate for the past forty years. The competing camps are legion: psycho- and socio-linguists, personal growth advocates, educational psychologists, postmodernists, feminists, New Critics (and *new* New Critics), archetypalists, moral grammarians, whole-languagers, and phenomenologists — to mention only a few leading schools.[1] As a result, anyone writing a monograph about pedagogical theory and practice in English teaching in the late twentieth century had better explain himself — up front and quickly.

Because so much of our theory has come to us in recent decades with only the barest of frameworks — promising much and delivering little — it is worth taking a closer look at the issue of theory itself. With or without theory, teachers still have to decide, whatever else is whirling about them beyond the classroom walls, what questions ought to be asked (or not asked) when grade tens open *Huckleberry Finn* on Monday morning. Such decisions, of course, are dependent upon the material under study and the goals society expects to be achieved when students encounter it. In the case of English literature, the materials have traditionally been made up of written texts in a variety of types and formats: sonnet, novel, magazine article, book review, Shakespearean play. The goals to be addressed as students deal with such texts have, until recent years, been surprisingly stable, varying little on syllabi across the English-speaking world.[2] These goals include the use of imaginative literature in assisting students to learn to read (initially, in primary school) and from there to develop their reading skills by getting their teeth into progressively more challenging texts. As this enterprise proceeds, related skills and abilities are folded in: students talk about texts read, write about them, and produce approximations of their own: poems, stories, essays. Reading, talking and writing: the fundamental trivium of literacy and, perhaps, the insignia of success in adult life.

These, then, have been the traditional givens for any English curriculum across the K-to-12 spectrum. And while each is fraught with controversy and contradiction, they do provide a steady focus for pedagogical argument. Further, any theory dealing with English teaching must take into account the nature of the thing being taught and what's done with it, by both teachers and students. This seems simple enough, but it isn't, for reading and writing involve much more than skill sets or problematical topics in the curriculum. Written texts, especially literary ones, and the interpretive processes they entail don't lend themselves to easy description. Yet if they are not described and understood clearly, there is little chance that we can ever effectively teach them.

We have to know what a poem or novel or essay *is*, and what accomplished readers themselves *do* when they confront, interpret and deploy such texts in the world. Only when we answer these questions, can we ask how the presence of a teacher and a systematic programme of studies might assist young, naive readers to reach adult levels of competency and, in doing so, absorb the values embedded in imaginative literature and apprehend the uses of advanced literacy.

It is, unfortunately, these very values and uses that are the flashpoint for recent public debate. As a result they too often overshadow the necessary prior discussion of the thing that is being valued and used. Novels and poems are, of course, studied in English courses because they contain valuable cultural content or prompt students to discuss pressing social issues.[3] They may also be treated as fodder for systematic training in deconstructing texts or recognizing logical fallacies, should these skills be deemed an overriding imperative in a dangerous and uncertain world. What is important to understand is that novels and poems are not always composed with such ends principally in mind. Equally important — and the core argument of this book — is that sophisticated interpretive abilities can best be advanced in students when these texts are read in the same spirit in which they were written. Moreover, if society expects its young people to learn to write in part by trying their hand at composing poetry and fiction, treating the latter as mere containers for sociological content, cultural history, or latent intertextual conspiracies will not benefit the neophyte author; more than likely it will induce terminal writer's cramp. It will also undermine any serious social benefits to be had from the reading of literature; such as, the vicarious experience of other people and places; an understanding of one's self in relation to these; and the growth of self-esteem that comes with the successful and satisfying interpretation of poems and stories, and the ability to discuss them with peers and others.

What *Teaching English* attempts to do is to return to some first-order questions about what literary texts actually are and how we come to know them, and in a way that is accessible to busy practitioners and productive of sound principles of teaching. In opening up these questions, I am acutely aware that the details of the debate about, say, poetry and the reading process are too abstruse and numerous to be revisited minutely. Nevertheless, the seminal work of Coleridge, Northrop Frye, Susanne Langer, George Steiner, Frank Smith, Don Holdaway, James Britton, Lev Vygotsky and Michael Polanyi — among others — must be acknowledged if any account of what I have called "aesthetic reading and poetic writing" is to be clear and defensible. For it is the *aesthetic* import of reading imaginative literature and the *poetic* aspect of writing fiction, poetry and drama that will be the focus of attention, elaboration and justification throughout the book, along with the most appropriate means of teaching them. What I have tried to do wherever possible is to consolidate and summarize the findings of these thinkers in a manner that, while cutting corners and sanding down nuance, remains readable and not too distortive of the original. I have added endnotes only where further reference and elaboration seem warranted, but it should be understood that almost every major claim I make has its origin elsewhere.

Chapter 1 introduces a hypothetical model for how we read any printed text, a theory that draws heavily upon the work of Smith and Polanyi. Then the hypothesized "normal" process is tested against the specific demands made upon the reader by the text of a poem. Do we have to adjust our normal reading process to accommodate any of the aesthetic features traditionally associated with poetry? Here I draw on my own experience as a composer and reader of verse to propose an aesthetic-reading model, and then try it out on a sample poem as it might be read by a grade-twelve student — first normally (non-aesthetically) and then aesthetically.

Chapter 2 takes a step back from the hands-on analysis to explore the nature of the thing itself — the poem — in an effort to establish and accurately define the aesthetic, and to do so in view of the many prominent, competing theories. Once again, some middle way between a recapitulation of the critical debates of the twentieth century and a simplistic manifesto has been attempted. The emphasis throughout this section is upon what makes a poem-text aesthetic as opposed to non-aesthetic, because that is the critical point in the contemporary controversy over the (undue?) influence that imaginative literature is purported to exert upon credulous students — whether it's the impact of explicit chauvinist or racist content or the hidden and lethal subtext exposable only through rigorous deconstruction.

Having offered a definition of poem as aesthetic text and tied it to the process of aesthetic reading introduced in chapter 1, we turn to the next logical question: what pedagogical principles can be derived from this prior theory, principles that may inform teaching and engender viable workaday methods? Six such principles are put forward and explained in light of the governing theory and competing notions. The last two sections of chapter 2 suggest specific teaching methods and lessons, along with a select bibliography of resources that are consistent with an aesthetic approach to teaching poetry.

With a notion of aesthetic reading and its potential in the English curriculum expounded and illustrated, chapter 3 looks at fiction in the same way: defining what it is, explaining how we might think about teaching it, and presenting sample lesson plans and resources. With much of the analysis and definition of the aesthetic having already been done for poetry, the discussion here of a theory of fiction, the process of reading it, and methods for teaching it focusses mainly on the differences between poetry and fiction as aesthetic texts.

Chapter 4 deals, in similar sequence, with what poetic writing is, what that tells us about a suitable pedagogy, and what actual lessons might look like. The poetic writing process is as unique and prototypal as aesthetic reading: to know one is to understand the other. In carrying out this analysis, it proved useful to review the conceptual muddle occasioned by the introduction of expressive-writing pedagogy in the 1970s and the all-pervasive practices of Writing Process in the 1980s.

Chapter 5 examines the flawed theory of the Writing Process movement to illustrate the inevitable consequences when teaching practice is derived from poorly conceptualized and untested assumptions about writing and writers. Conversely, the point is made that sound theory and related teaching principles are worth the effort to understand and apply them.

I must emphasize that the sample lessons and teaching suggestions given throughout are meant to be examples only, though some attempt has been made to include items across the K-to-12 curriculum.

This monograph is not intended to be a detailed handbook (a number of these are listed in the resource sections) nor is it a ground-clearing work of epistemology and literary criticism. It borrows from the latter and points tactfully towards the former.

Some readers may be wondering why so little attention has been paid thus far to the arguments of deconstructionists, post-structuralists and other postmodernists and related assaults on the old-fashioned ways of treating imaginative literature. There are two reasons for this. First and foremost, despite the prodigious efforts of many of these critics to include the arts, and imaginative literature in particular, in their general theory of intertexuality — in which the rhetoric of a sonnet by Donne can be read in the same way as the purple prose of a travel brochure — the recognition of politically and socially embedded aspects of literary texts and the reader's response to their aesthetic character remain parallel and complementary activities. We cannot claim that novels by definition have no political-social content, overt or otherwise, nor can we beg, for poems, immunity from deconstructive analysis merely because we think they are primarily aesthetic creations. Conversely, we ought to be skeptical of an analytical procedure that, in its zeal to unpack the hidden hazards of every text in the world, can find no legitimate place for a kind of experience known intimately, and attested to, by human beings everywhere: the *frisson* of inexpressible feeling that a poem or play or painting brings uniquely to each of us. Umberto Eco, no stranger to postmodern theory and practice, describes the necessity of our accepting both the open/skeptical stance of postmodern intertextuality and the closed/moral stance of literature in this way:

> If you had *War and Peace* in a hypertextual, interactive CD-ROM, you could rewrite your own story according to your desires. You could invent innumerable "War and Peaces" where Pierre Besuchov succeeds in killing Napoleon or, according to your penchant, Napoleon definitely defeats General Kutusoz.
>
> Alas, with an already written book whose fate is determined by irrepressible authorial decision, we cannot. We are obliged to accept the laws of fate and to realize that we are unable to change destiny. A hypertextual and interactive novel allows us to practice freedom and creativity, and I hope that such an inventive practice will be implemented in the schools of the future. But the already and definitely written *War and Peace* doesn't confront us with the unlimited possibilities of our imagi-

nations, but with the severe laws governing life and death ... There are books that we cannot rewrite because their function is to teach us about necessity, and only if they are respected as such can they provide us with such wisdom.[4]

Any attempt, however, to justify the teaching of imaginative literature by arguing its case solely in the light of postmodernist critiques is doomed to failure. George Steiner points this out in his seminal work, *Real Presences*. One by one he examines the various defenses that have been made over the past thirty years on behalf of the arts and their special place in the pantheon of texts. And one by one he illustrates that no telling argument can be made against the secularism of Derrida and company. There appears to be no sanctuary for the poem, no fine and private place for the novel. But, of course, millions of people continue to read novels as novels, persist in attending poetry readings, and naively allow themselves to be mesmerized by *Hamlet* or *Lear* on the Stratford stage. In short, despite the apparent triumph of postmodernism's understanding of knowledge, there remains a phenomenon yet to be explained: why *do* people continue to approach works of art on their own terms? What do they expect to derive from the encounter? Simply put, Steiner, not unlike Eco, suggests that most of the time we go to literature in the *expectation of meaning*, in the belief that we will find a coherence not otherwise knowable — a real presence. Readers of literature, then, are believers – before and during the event. Thus Steiner is able to begin his own argument with this arresting paragraph:

> [This essay] ... proposes that any coherent understanding of what language is and how language performs, that any coherent account of the capacity of human speech to communicate meaning and feeling is, in the final analysis, underwritten by the assumption of God's presence. I will put forward the argument that the experience of aesthetic meaning in particular, that of literature, of the arts, of musical form, infers the necessary possibility of this "real presence." The seeming paradox of a "necessary possibility" is, very precisely, that which the poem, the painting, the musical composition are at liberty to explore and to enact.[5]

Teaching English begins by accepting this general notion of what imaginative literature is and why we ought to approach it as something real and unique. It excludes much contemporary writing that questions such notions as presence and coherence. I believe that, for those millions of 'believers' out there, and their teachers, the English curriculum must include uninterrupted time and inviolable space for the patient study of imaginative literature and its aesthetic impact — for its "necessary possibility" and its "severe laws governing life and death." Only by doing so, will we, in Eco's words, "reach a higher state of intellectual and moral freedom."[6]

1

How We Read

The Process of Reading

One of the fundamental problems facing anyone attempting to describe how we read a poem, a story or a novel is that we still do not have an adequate account of how reading of any kind takes place. What follows is an hypothesis and a model about reading in general (i.e., normal reading), and aesthetic reading in particular. At this early stage of my argument, I will explicate the model in outline only, as the subsequent discussion of aesthetic reading and poetic writing will provide opportunities for elaboration and illustration. This model has been derived partly from my own experience of three decades spent teaching and observing student readers and writers, but it is also indebted to the work of Frank Smith, Michael Polanyi and Don Holdaway.[1]

When we begin to read we are usually aware that we are attempting to read something quite specific: an editorial, short story, poem, or lead item in our morning newspaper. In so doing we make particular adjustments to the general way we derive meaning from the squiggles on the page. It is this kind of adjustment that will occupy our attention throughout chapters 1 to 3.

As Smith has demonstrated, efficient readers attend to or focus upon the actual print (letters and words) as little as possible. In fact, once beginning readers move beyond the syllable-by-syllable and word-by-word phase of decoding (and for most children this happens very early on), they are only peripherally aware of letters and individual words because they are already grouping words (chunking) as their syntactical context dictates, and predicting, a phrase or two ahead, the words to come and meaning expected.[2] They do so naturally, because the cumulative imperative of meaning making prompts them to. What makes readers more efficient in general is their increasing ability to predict meaning; that is, in the actual cognitive process of reading itself, the reader is able to keep items like letters, words, syntactical units and chunks of meaning at the periphery of conscious awareness while focussing consciously on the evolving flow of thought and content. In the most efficient reading process, readers read through what we may loosely call the surface features, keeping them as much as possible at the periphery of consciousness (what Polanyi refers to as the zone of tacit awareness) because the *focal* task in the conscious part of the mind is not literal decoding, but rather the active pursuit of meaning. More directly, the efficient reader is always asking, "What is being said here? Where is this leading?" — and getting answers.

The cognitive mechanics here are what Polanyi calls 'from-to' processing. We read *from* the textual cues (that hover at the edge of awareness only) *to* the focus of our conscious attention (the flow of thought) and back again. The more we already know about letters, words, syntax and, later on, the myriad array of rhetorical devices (and the surface cues that trigger their presence and import), the more we can store and keep at the ready in the zone of tacit awareness. And by not having to pay conscious (and time-consuming) attention to such cueing, we can keep our mental sights focussed on the emergence of meaning, and on the element of prediction — which itself accelerates and intensifies the comprehension of text. And so, ideally, our mind hums along the line of print with millisecond and tacitly-confirmed glances at its surface features that feed inferences about meaning continuously to our consciousness.

But, of course, we are seldom in the ideal state for long. As soon as something on the surface disturbs our conscious attention — a word whose meaning we don't know immediately, a puzzling rhetorical cue — we instantly and naturally reverse the from-to process, shifting our focus to the surface and the problem there, while the flow of thought drifts to the periphery and mere tacit awareness. The efficient reader tries to resolve the disturbance by dipping quickly into any stored knowledge of rhetoric (diction, syntax, etc.) and coming up with either an answer or a decision to hold the question in abeyance (if it is deemed non-essential to the evolving flow of thought). Again, this process occurs in milliseconds, for the pressure to return to the more productive form of processing (from peripheral surface to focal flow of thought) is overwhelming. The more the reader already knows about language and rhetoric, the less disruptive these brief rhetoric blips will be. In addition to rhetoric blips there may also be minor thought blips. For even though the words and rhetorical cues may be being tacitly decoded, suddenly the thought doesn't make sense: where we assumed we were going is not where we have arrived. Once more the conscious focus may shift momentarily to the reader's ready store of life knowledge, and if it provides information that either resolves the query raised or suggests it may be held in abeyance, only a millisecond blip is noticed as the reader automatically readjusts the focus to the original flow of thought. As we will see later on, a tolerance for such disturbances and a sophisticated sense of when to hold them in abeyance — thus relying upon prediction and delayed confirmation — are the hallmarks of a maturing and successful reader.

These processes, then, constitute the most efficient way in which we can read a text. A less efficient form of reading takes place when we experience the sensation of a conscious *pause*, and abandon for a moment any rapid from-to processing while we search our easily accessible store of tacit knowledge for an answer to our query or decide to hold it in abeyance. If the pause is brief, we can resume normal processing with only a slight tremor of interruption. If pauses are too frequent or too long (two or three seconds, say, or more if we need to scour the tacit store deeply or flip back, literally or figuratively, to an earlier part of the text or, worse, look up a word in the dictionary or consult a footnote), the cumulative flow of thought (i.e., ongoing comprehension) may be seriously impaired. If no resolution to a serious query is found in either the readily accessible store of knowledge or the deeper one, the reader may decide to abandon the enterprise.

When a reader has finished reading a whole text, he or she should be left with a sense of closure; of having had all questions (self-raised) answered; of having pursued the flow of meaning through whatever cumulative phases it has taken; and, in general, ought to feel that some whole thought has been grasped through a progressive comprehension of parts.

The actual process of reading — even of the most straightforward text — is, of course, many times more complex than I have indicated. Not only are we pursuing meaning by reading through as much of the surface as we can to satisfy the pressing need to know what is being said to us moment by moment, but we are, tacitly again, building up an image or picture or sense of the *thought*: "What is this *really* saying? Is there some larger point? Point of view? Argument?" This is what Langer would call virtual thought (that is, an attempt by the reader to replicate what he or she understands to be the essence and intention of the original 'idea' in the author's head).

In reading any completed text, the notion of intention, of a voice (the author's or a persona) speaking to *us*, and of some eventual outcome or closure is as significant as our effort to grasp the millisecond by millisecond inflow of immediate meanings. This larger sense of intentional thought is itself kept mostly tacit, but, again, there will be occasion to pause and *focus* on it: "Where *is* this going? I can't believe *that*!" Amazingly, readers feel that all this is happening simultaneously because the focal-peripheral inversion is occurring so rapidly. It is only in beginning readers, or in those whose reading experience is limited (impoverishing the readily available tacit knowledge of rhetoric), or when the text's content is beyond our store of life knowledge that the automatic processing breaks down, and shows itself to be one that must be learned.

Reading Poetry

Although I suspect that all forms of efficient reading enact this basic focal-peripheral processing (it is hard to conceive of it not happening something like this), it is when we test the model against certain specific types of text that serious questions arise. For example, the model seems consistent with how many of us go about comprehending an account in our community newspaper about an accident or flood or robbery — in a straight-ahead narrative-expository format. No finger will be needed to wobble along under the line of print word by word, for most of us already know how to keep individual words at the periphery of attention, while we avidly pursue the sensational facts unfolding in phrase, sentence and paragraph (short) in a format as comfortable as our slippers. This acquired familiarity with newsstory text will aid prediction, as will any relevant local knowledge we might have of the people and places therein. The vocabulary of such journals is designed to be broadly accessible, so that the only major pauses are likely to be over content items (an acquaintance's name pops up in the text and initiates a reflective pause; a strange technical term asserts itself, but is skipped over as non-pertinent or held in abeyance until it can be added in or edited out later on according to the reader's needs). At the end of the account, the individual parts are known, as well as any rounding-off comment (implied or stated). Closure and a sense of full comprehension have been satisfactorily achieved — such satisfaction having been determined by the *reader*, in that the original purpose for perusing the passage (and continuing to do so) has been met.[3] While most texts signal — in their structure, content and setting — a specific intention, it is always the individual reader who decides how much of it will be respected, a critical factor in any theorizing about the education of readers.

So far, so good. But is reading a narrative-expository text in a familiar setting (the daily paper) the same experience as reading a poem that appears, say, as filler between two theme-units of short stories in a grade-eight anthology (a lamentably common occurrence)? In this case, there is little or no guiding context as to purpose or intention. Let us assume for the sake of argument that Martin, a naive reader in grade eight (he is inexperienced in reading or writing poetry, and uncertain in general about his reading abilities), approaches such a poem-text. He suspects it is a poem (he spots the stanza-chunks and notices a rhyme), but lacks any specific ways of adjusting his customary all-purpose reading process. So he proceeds to read the lines of the poem as if they were lines of print in a newspaper, silently reading from the surface towards the expected flow of thought, with the parts of the text successively unfolding in his mind — let us say, a series of word-pictures and some sort of statement about them at the end. When asked to tell his teacher what the poem is about, Martin dutifully recounts the sequence of word-pictures (as best he can in his own words) and concludes by merely reciting the statement-comment in the poem's last line. If prodded to go further, he may even venture an opinion as to what the final statement might be suggesting about the word-pictures. Certainly, as a reader, Martin himself is satisfied because he was able to comprehend, in a normal reading fashion, pretty much all of the words and the literal images they evoked, and he realized that the last line was meant as some form of overview and closure.

Has the poem been read? Technically, it has, because Martin did not abandon the attempt or suffer frustration. He pursued meaning through to the end, was able to give a reasonable summary of the content, and even guessed at the implied meaning of the last line. But did he read the text as a poem? No. And here is the problem: a poem is above all an *aesthetic* text and begs to be read on its own terms. The differences between aesthetic texts — poems, short stories, novels and play-scripts — and non-aesthetic ones (all the others) will be explored in great detail in the coming chapters. At this point, the critical distinction to be made in terms of the reading process we are discussing is that in a text designed and intended to be read aesthetically the surface features are so bound up in its meaning that they ought not to be read through or kept tacit at the periphery of awareness while the important task of capturing the cumulative flow of thought is kept focal and conscious. As we shall see, in initial encounters with a poem-text, the reader must do almost the opposite: let the rhythm, metre, sound effects (rhyme, consonance, repetition) and arresting metaphors remain in tremulous balance with the flow of thought, for ultimately the flow of thought must incorporate them. In our example above, Martin took no notice of the rhyme or any connotative aspect of the imagery (a staple of many lyric poems) or the possible pattern of images that might prove critical in understanding the overview comment at the end — either in the tacit processing of the surface or in the evolution of his sense of where the meaning of the whole poem was taking him. For example, could the final comment perhaps be ironic? Might it urge us to read the poem again from another angle? And so on.

Moreover, poems do not yield meaning through the slow accretion of parts, particularly lyric poems, which we will emphasize here because they are the thing itself: pure aesthetic text. In poetry the whole is always more than the sum of its parts, with much of the meaning derived from gestalt-like leaps where mood, tone, sound, and poem-patterning (poem-grammar) come together to create sudden insights. And so, effective poems are always non-synonymous; that is, they can't be adequately summarized in other words or ordinary prose. And because their meaning is in large part a form-of-feeling (to paraphrase Susanne Langer),[4] it resides in our sensibility even though it arrives there through the cognitive process of reading.

Finally, the amount of prior experience stored tacitly in the minds of young students for use in responding to and comprehending poetry is dozens, perhaps hundreds, of times bigger and more wide-ranging than that for use in reading expository or argumentative texts. In the next chapter, I will discuss how and why this should be so, but the fact that it is, is vital to our understanding of why it is that poem-texts, when approached aesthetically, are both familiar and comprehensible to students — even (and especially) in primary school. Miraculously, most children arrive in kindergarten richly prepared to read and write the most complex form of human expression.

Indeed, having such a rich prior experience, stored deeply but available to the zone of tacit awareness, is a fundamental prerequisite for reading a lyric poem. The aesthetic reading process is many times more complicated than the reading process we bring to, say, a news story, a travel brochure, or an E-mail note from a friend. For a start, we have to be able to take in the poem's rhetoric, its poem-grammar.

As well, the flow of thought here is really more like a sense of immediate and evolving feeling and thought bound together. We do not, or should not, try to separate the two, for poems produce them together and at once. More accurately, then, they will be referred to as the flow of *feeling-thought*.

Once again, the reading of the surface (words, syntactical units, obvious phrase- and line-structure) is ideally peripheral and tacit, but remains so only momentarily. For unlike the reading of expository prose (i.e., what I earlier called the normal reading process), where the reader's eye and brain chunk as much meaning as possible peripherally and feed the chunks to the focal task of pursuing the flow of thought, the efficient reader of poetry will subvocalize or silently hear the words and their phrasing *before* they are fed to the conscious, focal task. Attention will be paid to the literal meaning and to rudimentary syntax, of course, but since the basic unit of the poem is the shaped phrase and/or the metrical line rather than the prose sentence, the ongoing subvocalization will enunciate or 'perform' the surface structure in phrases and lines. This can be done naturally and kept tacitly peripheral because the required information is fed in from prior experience with poem-texts. Hence, the more focal and conscious task is to make meaning out of the "heard" phrasings, themselves generated from the surface of the text (something that Martin above failed to do).

There will, however, be no sense of a single flow of feeling-thought, for the subvocalizations provide the interpretive inner voice of the reader with crafted phrasings set in sound clusters, with pounding or lulling rhythms, with iterative consonance and rhyme, and with newly minted images and metaphors, all of which bring with them a physicality, a weight of being, as it were. In part the reader's mind always asks, "What am I seeing here? Where is this going?" but in aesthetic reading the poem-rhetoric (that is, the array of devices indigenous to verse) arrives simultaneously with the semantic import and insists on remaining integral to the feeling-thought that lies at the heart of all lyric poetry and serves as its primary purpose. Initially, there is an intense from-to processing that the reader feels to be happening all at once. Then, of course, the mind switches in milliseconds to the surface for fresh linguistic-rhetorical information, subvocalizes it and carries on with the process. Where, then, is the ongoing flow of meaning? Surely readers do not render themselves semi-comatose and just let the sounds and rhythms wash over them (as they might at a symphony concert) and allow all meaning to drift, at best, into the zone of tacit awareness.[5]

They do not. Certainly in the first or second encounter with a lyric poem, the physical shape and particularity of the poetic effects will exert a powerful connotative-associative influence, and such effects produce in the reader moments of aesthetic pleasure. (These are *noticed* moments, the kind that prompt a gratuitous "Ah" from the reader, for there is always a tacit hum of aesthetic pleasure in the reading experience as a whole, indefinable but as familiar as that which accompanies our response to a song or a sonata.) The images, events and statements *are* denotative — they mean what they say (a fact that sometimes escapes students) — and, in combination with their aesthetic context, produce, as we go, moments of gestalt insight: glimpses into where the text is leading us and into the emergent shape of the feeling-thought it seeks to enact and embody. Any blips and brief pauses will, ideally, be aesthetic or insightful ones.

If they are not, then overt pauses — either to enjoy and relish a pleasingly crafted phrase or to query too explicitly an initially puzzling trope, syntactical inversion or neologism — are likely to subvert the flow of feeling-thought. In brief, because both the aesthetic features and the subtle feeling-thought features of a lyric poem are equally important to the overall meaning and pleasure (that is, reader satisfaction), on the first encounter or two with the text, readers will have to be not exactly comatose but nonetheless highly tolerant of unanswerable questions prompted by the structure or semantics. The double flow of comprehension (where meaning and rhetoric are bound together), the abrupt gestalts of insight, and unsought proddings from the tacit zone (which in aesthetic reading is more proactive and anticipatory) make it essential that pauses and explicit questing for resolution be kept to a minimum. Of course, even though, at the conclusion of a first reading, the reader's satisfaction is composed of a sense of aesthetic closure,[6] of having lived through a dynamic and shaped feeling-thought, the text can be immediately re-engaged and read again in a similar manner. Moreover, further readings may be instigated, ones that resemble to some degree the normal reading process.

All of this sounds so impossibly complicated that we might despair of teaching even talented English majors how to read a simple ballad. But it is so only when we try to tease such a cognitive process out of its tacit setting. As we shall see in chapter 2, much of the aesthetic reading process has become automatic or natural by the time most children enter kindergarten. The principal impediment to their deploying these skills as they learn to read independently is likely to be the kind of confusion that arises when the reading process used in comprehending non-aesthetic texts is erroneously applied to aesthetic ones — often with the connivance of the teacher.

It is time to look at a specific example in order to see how an aesthetic reading might differ from an unaesthetic one and how it is quite possible for a student reader to confuse the two in school. Here is a recent poem of mine about words and poetry itself:

The Word

> In Sunday school we sang
> of baby-Jesus in Bethlehem's hay,
> of cattle stunned in their stalls,
> of lambs whose precious blood
> God loved, and the sparrow's fall,
> we mouthed the Word-Made-Flesh
> that began it all ...
>
> O how we carolled our Christmas
> Wenceslaus / our kings
> of Orient and myrrh!
> our angels hearkening holy
> in a night so silent
> the snows could be heard
> vespering the virgin word.
>
> Ah, but then, in those
> first chanting Noels,
> we didn't know
> the Babe was Everychild:
> whose birth breathes the world
> back to its beginning.
>
> we didn't know
> we were singing
>   ourselves.

Let us assume that Mary, an intelligent but literal-minded grade-twelve student (who attended Sunday school until she was thirteen) is asked to read "The Word" on her own and write an interpretation of it. She approaches the text as she would any sort of expository or descriptive-expository piece. Reading from the surface she moves easily along the flow of thought:

> The poet is recalling her youth when she sang Christmas carols in Sunday school, like "Away in a Manger" with cows looking down on Jesus, and some hymns (I think "The Precious Blood of the Lamb" is one and so is "God Sees the Little Sparrow Fall") and they sing about the Word-Made-Flesh (whatever that is, the incarnation?) that began — what? — the world? Genesis? Anyway, the carol singing continues with "Good King Wenceslaus" and "We Three Kings" (should be frankincense, not orient) and "Silent Night" which reminds her of the Virgin Mary and snow (was there snow in Bethlehem?) and its — what? — *vespering?* (speaking? never heard of the word) the ... the birth of Jesus by Mary? Then the poet starts to tell us what she's getting at: when she was a kid singing carols she didn't know that baby Jesus was like all the babies who are fresh and new when they're born and it seems like a beginning all over again; in the last part the poet finally comes out with the theme, that the carollers were singing themselves — because they were children and really like the baby Jesus they were singing about, or something like that.

One could easily imagine a much less competent running précis of the poem. Much of the thought in it has been successfully inferred, even if it is in an early, inchoate form. But almost all of the poem's aesthetic aspect has been ignored or only marginally included as tacit information underpinning Mary's comprehension (e.g., she senses that "vespering" is unusual, perhaps metaphoric, and perhaps tied consonantally to "virgin word"). But what would Mary's first reading (or several similar rereadings) reveal if she had adopted an aesthetic posture towards the text?

If she had subvocalized the text, the sound effects and phrase shaping would have remained part of the focal processing, not the peripheral. The line break at "sang" (line 1) puts more emphasis on that verb in concert with the S alliteration throughout the line and its lilting rhythm — suggesting immediately that the singing was enjoyable, almost tactile. While line 2 seems straightforward, the use of "*baby*-Jesus" and the odd phrasing of "Bethlehem's hay" (tied to "baby" through the consonance of *b* and long-*a* and its own alliterative *h*em and *h*ay) adds weight to the images, while line 3, in alluding to the crèche scene, presents an alliterated phrase and line that surely produces an aesthetic jolt (blip or pause) and likely a gestalt insight (the pure *power* of the miracle they are beholding). The consonance effects and phrase/line shaping are presented as heard items, but it is not the conscious mind that reads alliteration or consonantal play or lilting rhythm, but rather the zone of tacit awareness from which flashes of pleasure and insight are flung into the stream of conscious feeling-thought as it evolves. The aesthetic text demands that we keep moving, allowing inkling and intimation to remain just that, while we prepare for the next set of phrasings from our peripheral scanning of the surface. This double jolt of pleasure and insight continues through to the last line of the poem.

Here, as an aesthetic reader, Mary would not only register the presence of a summing-up statement but, having permitted the aesthetic features of the poem to remain tied to the semantic unfolding, she would now know or tacitly infer that the phrase "singing / ourselves" was not meant as an expository theme statement but as an invitation for her to re-engage the poem in light of it and/or reflect upon the notion that the poem has already embodied or enacted that thought. The magic of the miracle surrounding the incarnation of the Holy Spirit in Jesus as represented in the singing of the carols is signalled in the verbal and tonal density and intricate consonance of "Chri*s*t*m*a*s* / Wence*s*laus," "angel*s h*earkening *h*oly," "*v*espe*r*ing the *v*i*r*gin wo*r*d," and the simple rhymes and assonance linking them (as in the carols?): "Noels," "angels," "stalls," "fall," "all," "kings," "hearkening," "beginning," "singing," "myrrh," "heard" and "world." So the notion that the children were singing themselves comes not as a surprise or a rounding off, but rather as a signature statement or coda of what has already been enacted (e.g., "Every*ch*ild" is linked by consonance to "*ch*anting" and "ours*elves*" to "no*els*"). What has been felt and intimated — the mystery of the flesh-spirit miracle — has been confirmed, and if those inklings have remained tacit, then the surprise of the last lines would send the aesthetic reader back for a re-engagement with the text: rereading it as above with a view to letting more of the embodied/enacted theme (i.e., its feeling-thought) reveal itself with its aesthetic elements still intact. Or, as we shall see in chapter 2, Mary might initiate a second reading of selected parts, itself governed and aided by the initial encounters.

The consequences of each type of reading — aesthetic and non-aesthetic — are as unequivocal as they are different. If Mary goes to the poem-text expecting to re-enact a unique conjunction of feeling and thought, and assents to read it in the way most appropriate to that end, she will not be disappointed. She may not be able to articulate all she knows after the event, but that possibility will have been accepted in advance. However, if she mistakes the poem-text for a discursive one, or even a sort of prosy description, she will automatically apply another process of comprehension (or do so by default), with an entirely different result. None of this is to say that having Mary go home and write an interpretation of "The Word" is an appropriate assignment under any circumstance (or, indeed, that the poem would be appropriate in a multicultural classroom), but having some prior notion that the text is a poem (and thus imaginative literature) and that poem-texts require of the reader both dispositional and cognitive-processing adjustments ought to assist teachers in making that decision. In sum, an understanding of the similarities and differences between these two reading processes, combined with a sure grasp of what poems are and do in the world, should lead us directly to the task of deriving general and specific teaching strategies for English.

***

Twenty-five years ago, the reading models proposed above and the use of specific examples to substantiate their validity would have been enough, in the least, to set the parameters for further debate and discussion, because the aesthetic aspects of poetry itself were not then in question among English teachers, nor was their importance seriously challenged. All that has changed; all of the basic tenets of belief about literature have been questioned, as Steiner has so eloquently noted: the concept of author, the referentiality of language, the high seriousness of poetry's purpose, the categorization of texts as aesthetic or otherwise and the values long associated with those beliefs. So it is that we must step back and try to define the terrain of being and knowing we call poetry. Simply put, we need to define what a poem uniquely is, and how that knowledge governs what we can say about how we ought to read it and how we might go about teaching others to do the same.

2

Aesthetic Reading: Poetry

The Thing Itself

Poetry is verse elevated to the precinct of art. It is necessary to distinguish between verse and poetry, not because they do not share elements and values, but because the term poetry in common parlance is applied metaphorically to several kinds of verbal, and even non-verbal, expression. For example, we might refer to a politician's eloquent address to Parliament or a novelist's stylish prose as poetic, and the moves of an ice hockey star may be described by an enthusiastic sportscaster as "poetry in motion." Rightly so, for the metaphor works in these instances. Similarly but not so critically, the term verse is often applied to rhyming doggerel — of the "Roses are red / Violets are blue" variety. But if we are to develop a definition of the kind of poetry we wish to teach in schools and one that will be clear enough to point us towards pedagogical theory and practice, we must begin with an examination of what constitutes verse, and proceed from there to the nature of poetry and the implications for teaching.

In its elementary state, verse is one of the three fundamental rhythms of human speech and written expression, the other two being the associative rhythm and the prose rhythm.[1] In its expressed forms — that is, the actual uses we make of it in our lives — verse is marked by pronounced metrical cadence and the deliberate deployment of consonance; i.e. rhyme; repetition of sounds, words and syntactical items; onomatopoeia. Long before writing and the exigency of epic, our forebears recognized the mnemonic value of verse, and even today we appreciate the aid to memory of "*i* before *e* except after *c*." Moreover, then or now, verse comes to us early and naturally. The very first forms of speech learned and used by any two-year-old are verse-shaped. The parent who endlessly repeats each baby utterance — often, and most productively, in an atmosphere of play, good humour and a boundless tolerance for error — is attuning the infant to the most significant elements of the mother tongue that will last it a lifetime. In brief, words as referents and as parts of syntactically entailed phrases are learned fundamentally in relation to their sounds, to the playfulness of their deployment, and to their connotative and affective value. While denotation ("There's Daddy, say 'daa-dee'!") is prior and necessary, it is embedded in and ideally inseparable from the intrinsic delight the child displays in repeating it (interminably!), in savouring its syllable sounds, and in recognizing the pleasure it brings to Daddy. The infant replicates the action in private play, joyously discovering its syntactic possibilities ("Daddy come," "Daddy go," "Where Daddy go?"), and the way it stimulates a mental image and the feeling it arouses even when the object is absent and there is no listener to reinforce and confirm: "Daddy driving car, driving car."

There is no mystery, then, that nursery rhymes, jingles and pattern stories are so well received and effortlessly reproduced in the child's own spontaneous acting out and role play, alone or with peers. The fact that music, mostly the kind of songs enjoyed by children, is also rooted in rhythm and suggests, or connotes, feelings is neither accidental nor incidental. And the importance of music and verse for teaching in preschool and kindergarten are richly demonstrated in the professional literature of the past forty years.[2]

The basic unit of the verse rhythm is the cadenced line, shaped metrically to the ear, and its connotative discretion: "Daddy come! Daddy come!" is both a set of excited verse-lines and syntactically rudimentary sentences. But metre, repetition, and connotative pleasure (that is, personal associations and intimated meanings), in the uttering and in its context, are more important than simple denotation and undeveloped grammar. It is much further on in a child's linguistic development that the essential unit of the prose rhythm, the sentence, develops and, as Frye has noted, becomes fully functional mainly in written prose and formal speech. The point here is that the verse rhythm and its additional quality of feeling are both fundamental and instinctively familiar to every child who learns to speak; and they are learned as an integral part of the acquisition of our mother tongue.

What this means is that poetry, or art-speech,[3] is not something to be taught or learned after we have perfected the proper sentence of ordinary prose-speech (whatever that is). Nor is it an art form or artifice so sophisticated and unnatural that it must be ladled out to children with adult circumspection and guarded gloss. Rather, it should be presented to them as a pleasurable variant of a language experience they already know and appreciate. This can only be so if we come to understand that poetry is the aesthetic use made by poets of the universal verse rhythm, and formalized in writing and print.

The use of verse to aid memory and the affective power of its repetitions were, of course, recognized by the societies that produced *The Iliad* and *Beowulf*. The metrical line, the set phrase and its variations, the chiming of repeated sounds, the imagery which aids visualization — all intensify the emotional impact of the story. These adjuncts of the verse rhythm, already familiar to the listeners, soon became the stock aesthetic components of the art-speech of epic. The musical accompaniment of lute or lyre was just as natural an addition as melody was to a mother's lullaby words; and the need of the performer to remember previous variants (and the open invitation to improvise upon them) resulted in the shaped, cadenced phrase and metrical line becoming staple devices. In the same way, lyric verse evolved from, or at the same time as, the song; rhyme, rhythmic phrasing, imagery and recurring sound patterns were — and are — integral to its effects. Put another way, a poem's meaning must include not merely its literal content (Achilles' pout or Beowulf's battle with Grendel), but its rhythms, metrics, rhymes, repetitions, consonance, set phrases, any or all of which could qualify the meaning of the "content." Those who write poetry, read it, and teach it must recognize that this is so.[4] But for those struggling with the complexity of the notion and its apparently bizarre logic (for example, how *can* iambic pentameter *mean*?), a lucid theory and plausible explanation is in order.

A poem is a non-discursive, presentational form of expression.[5] Because it is comprised of words with referential and denotative quality in a recognizable syntax (however distorted for effect), we are apt to mistake it for an eccentric discursive text. After all, the basic unit of prose discourse is the sentence, whose meaning obtains in the logical relations of its syntactic elements (e.g., its subject and predicate). Without the sentence, without subject and predication, human thought would be impossible, we assume. And so, when a poem appears before us or is recited at us, we immediately register its nouns and verbs, and we conjure up the picture suggested by the objects and actions to which they refer, as we do in everyday conversation or in scanning the morning paper. Certainly, that is what Martin and Mary did in chapter 1: they read the assigned poem as ordinary discourse. Mind you, it *was* somewhat eccentric because the sentences were chopped up into arbitrary lines and squeezed into stanzas, and several rhymes chimed tantalizingly in the background.

But when the metrics, rhyming, and stanza-chunking of rudimentary verse are elevated to art-speech, they become so much more than containers for discursive thought. As poems, they present what they communicate: they enact or embody it. What is conveyed is the thing itself: words, sentences, rhythms, stanzas, sounds — enmeshed in and comprising a pattern, a whole shape with every one of its parts still extant and shimmering. And somewhere just below or above or infinitely interior is an intimation of truth, a phenomenon that I have elsewhere called "the myth alive."[6] Langer tells us that the purest form of presentational art is music — symphony, sonata, tone poem — where there are only free-floating, associative meanings, and we may choose to devote our attention to the swerve and jolt of the feeling it renders. We are not necessarily awash in unadulterated emotion, however. For a symphony, like all presentational forms, enacts a particular sequence and quality of feeling, one that can be re-experienced at will, but whose form is constant, the flow and articulation of its parts ever to be repeated in the same groove in real time. Poems are problematic in this regard only because they do use words and sentences with statement-like implications. Nonetheless, poems are, as Langer insists, *non*-discursive, presentational forms. Like a symphony, they provide a score which, when re-enacted by a reader, calls up a fixed sequence of images, sounds, and a peculiar quality of feeling.

Poems, then, are about the shape and quality of feeling, its contours, its affective landscape. They are not mere incitement to unspecified emotion precisely because they *have* a shape, an order of "events," one that can be revisited or replayed but not summarized in the way that most discursive writing can be. Even so, why place a high value on poems? While important in our lives, feeling is surely lower on the scale of human endeavour than thought?

Not so, for poetry is itself a category of thought in that a poem presents to us, in real time, the opportunity to re-experience a feeling unique to it. And because a poem is a public document, fixed in form and infinitely repeatable, it serves us as a *thought* as surely as does a syllogism. Even when poetry appears to be overtly discursive, like the famous opening lines of Eliot's "Burnt Norton" ("Time present and time past / Are both perhaps present in time future"), its declarations are usually incantatory, runic, epigrammatic, afloat on a sea of rhythm and qualifying consonance. In such a way do metre and sound-clusters, rhetorical and stanzaic patterning, and the palpability of words in inexorable order come to have meaning: they shape and present a unique thought about human feeling so that it can only be understood by being performed. There are no thoughts distinct from what is to be felt.

That not every reader gets precisely the same thought as another should not detract from the larger question of a poem's status and general effect. Discursive prose is no different: learned tomes are still being written to explain the writings of Plato or Marx to us once and for all. When we read a poem, then, we are in quest of a feeling-thought — a unique node of feeling — and we find it only by replaying the "score" provided us. Like other more discursive thoughts, we can possess it, let it dwell in us, use it to think with, or enter into public discussion about what it means to us. But we must carry it about *whole* and, as occasion demands, revisit it with courtesy if we are to glimpse again the vital myth humming in the particulars.[7] In this light, imaginative literature can be defined as a repository of feeling-thoughts, as culturally significant as accounts of our history or works of philosophy. Moreover, its roots in the verse rhythm we all learned in the nursery and bruited noisily in the schoolyard means that our access to its more sophisticated canon ought to be easy, natural and progressive.

This description of poetry and its purpose is neither new nor original. It is as ancient as Aristotle and his impossible probabilities. But if it is a true description, everything else follows.

How much of this whole, this felt truth, is the poet aware of and intending? If a covenant of courtesy ought to obtain between writer and reader, then intention becomes a critical question. The poet composes with an embryonic and barely conscious sense of some whole meaning (that encompasses both feeling and form together – one leading the other interchangeably), towards which the parts as they emerge on paper are contributing, and at some point the imperative of closure asserts itself, and the whole is complete. And, as Coleridge insisted, it is always more than the sum of its parts. Shelley compared the whole thought that propelled the parts of a poem into existence to a fading coal, and like most writers he realized that the resultant structure of words was a mere approximation of what prompted it. When poets speak of this phenomenon of creating, it is often in metaphor and sometimes with embarrassment because the process feels magical, yet appears in hindsight to be mechanical and pedestrian. Nevertheless, we have enough credible testimony from them over centuries and cultures to take as a given that their intention is to capture in words what is ineffable but worth approximating in the most precise form of expression we have: the art-speech of the poem.

But poems are not symphonies, not even quartets. Symphonies are performed *for* us. Poems must be read, and reading, as we have seen, is an intense, cognitive activity of astonishing complexity. It is time to look at what is required of the reader if a poem-text is to be experienced aesthetically. First, our definition of a poem implies a particular relationship between the text and the person reading it, or, if you like, between the poet's sense of what he meant in the poem and the reader's approximation of it as a consequence of any interpretive efforts. The poem presents something utterly new but with enough familiarity of language and referenced experience to induce both a perception of significant novelty ("I hadn't felt it in quite that way") and the shock of recognition ("Ah, and so it is!"). Once we acknowledge and willingly accept the aesthetic purpose of the work, we are able, and must, enter into a covenant with the poem's creator, one that is as simple as it is contentious in the postmodern universe.

A poem-text is to be approached "courteously" (Steiner's term), that is, with that willing suspension of disbelief Coleridge urged upon us almost two hundred years ago. Included here is an expectation of meaning, a belief that coherencies exist — created in and of the words themselves — and a tacit agreement that the poet had something real and unique in mind when setting out, which each new reader is invited to pursue. Whether that real meaning closely approximates in the reader the deliberate intention of the original or varies wildly from reader to reader is not germane here, for what is paramount to the act of aesthetic reading is that the reader accept that the poet creates a meaning by aesthetic means. In extending the poet and poem such a courtesy, the reader acknowledges that the text presented for re-enactment and interpretation has been composed aesthetically and begs a reading in those terms only.

The full meaning of a poem or novel (however elusive or ambiguous) necessarily involves its aesthetic elements and the complexities of the parts-whole phenomenon.[8] Aesthetic readers accept that a direct engagement with the poem's rhythm and consonance is obligatory; they bring, insofar as anyone can, only those parts of their own experience and value-system incited by the exacting references of the words and metaphors in the poem itself. This is what Mary attempted when she abandoned her normal reading process and adopted an aesthetic one to begin her re-engagement with "The Word."

Of course, this is a tall order, and the subject of endless debate in recent critical and professional literature.[9] Readers, it must be conceded, are *invited* to bring to the poem their own experience, as technically skilled decoders and as citizens of the world who have lived and felt and judged. At the same time it is hoped they will attend to the precise meaning of the poem's words, their aesthetic effects and their unique way of making meaning. But, once again, the *degree* to which readers are able to curtail the random and unproductive application of their own experience is not as critical to an appropriate form of aesthetic reading as is the *willingness to attempt* a suspension of disbelief. We try to do so because we go to aesthetic texts expecting that their aesthetic quality has the potential to provide us with a kind of knowledge and sense of coherence we can find in no other phenomena, and these texts require such a suspension in order to bring that prize into our presence. If we do not believe such knowledge and coherence exists in poems (and many postmodernists and the contemporary breed of positivist do not[10]), then we have no reason to go there or concern ourselves with learning how to become courteous readers. Oh, there *are* other reasons — biographical, psychoanalytical, historical, ideological — but each of them excludes or distorts the aesthetic primacy of the poem's way of meaning.

In emphasizing such a suspension of disbelief, we have noted the importance to be placed upon the reader's willingness to act in this fashion, for no one can make us suspend disbelief, a fact that Steiner seizes on to introduce the notion of freedom implied in the writer-reader relationship.[11] Equally important is the term suspension, for it suggests a deliberate delay for some purpose, and not, as some would have it, a mindless surrender of our own values and experiences in fawning favour of the poet's. When we choose to take up the role of aesthetic reader in the presence of a poem, we agree to defer any general or premature application of our rooted prior experience, whether it be rhetorical or personal in nature, in order to engage the meaning of the poem as it unfolds. We do so because the temptation to respond to the discursive elements of the text (the literal content of words and images in their syntactical setting) immediately upon recognizing them can distract our attention from the presentational elements. For the latter must be allowed to speak to us first, before any discursive analysis begins. It is not that we should ignore the obvious content on our initial reading(s), but rather that we let it undulate comfortably below the insistent urgings of the poem's aesthetic qualities. Put more simply, we ought not to stop in the midst of a first read-aloud to puzzle over the dictionary meaning of a word or attempt a premature guess or two as to what the poem is *really* about, while lending but half an ear to a pertinent rhyme, an evolving metaphor, or an unexpected shift in tone.

Surely this is what is meant when we say that the reader re-enacts what the poet has enacted in the words of the poem. We build up not merely a picture of the events that the text conjures up, but a sense of the drama that it plays out for us again and again. It is as if we are watching a film loop, with image and dramatic montage reverberating in us until the parts of our own experience called up by the image and flow are themselves shaped in a way they never were before. (And herein may lie the true subversiveness of poetry.)

Once we have satisfied ourselves that we have grasped some sense of the whole structure and drama, we may then, should we wish to do so, proceed to a more focussed attention on parts.[12] But any such analysis, as we shall see below, must be done in light of any initial tacit understandings, with a view to intensifying and elaborating them while remaining under their governance. Even here, private associations and idiosyncratic opinions will be most productive if their relationship to aesthetic elements is understood.

For example, if Mary had initially adopted an aesthetic-reading posture for "The Word," her familiarity with the Christian context and allusions of the poem would have permitted her not only to pick up the potential import of the references to carol singing and the incarnation, but also to have them call up specific affective associations from her own childhood experience, associations prompted by the allusions in the poem and the rhythm and sound clusters through which they are *presented*. Conversely, she would have delayed the premature application of any knowledge about Christian doctrine; For example, the implied similarity between Christ's incarnation and every child's is not exactly orthodox, and might easily have coloured Mary's response to the last stanza to the point where subsequent re-engagements with the text would be compromised. At some point, of course, Mary or her teacher will want to raise the doctrinal question, as the text itself invites the reader to. But, first, the full connotative impact of the images, allusions, sound clusters, and subtle ironies of the poem's thought should hold sway.

Finally, it is *disbelief* that we are asked to defer, not our own deep-seated and cherished convictions. The poem begs us to re-enact its feeling-thought. The way we have been defining a poem urges us towards a reading model that encourages the text to be re-enacted by a reader whose responses, though governed by an aesthetic covenant, can now be invited in as an essential participant. For example, Keats's "On First Looking into Chapman's Homer" remains a poem-text until a reader makes it a poem. The idealized original in the poet's mind may be replicated by an infinite number of reader approximations; that none approach the original is of no consequence (even the poet's didn't), provided that the pursuit is taken up in the same spirit and to the same purpose. Like stout Cortez, in Keats's sonnet, we will want to stand on Darien's peak and imagine the magnitude of the sight that silenced him and his men.

Students are often disappointed when teachers cannot promise them that somewhere there is a best reading or perfect interpretation — a notion that unfortunately (and perhaps inadvertently) distorts and depreciates the reader's role in re-enacting, as best he can, the poem in the text, knowing that personal associations and feelings are bound to be part of any approximation.[13] Again, it is the spirit and purpose of the pursuit that matter most. Similarly, what was missing in the well-intentioned efforts of New Criticism was a recognition of the role that tacit understanding plays in our initial and repeated engagements.[14] The New Critics did some dazzling interpretive dances for us, and many of their inquisitions yielded important analytical techniques, but how impoverished is their reference to the subtle effects of sound and to rhythm (as opposed to metre) and how narrow their infatuation with dense texture, ironic tension, and erudite conceits.

The dispositional adjustments demanded of the aesthetic reader sound complicated enough to require some sort of sustained clinical programme for would-be students of poetry, but, as in the case of the primary verse rhythm that underpins poetry, such adjustments occur early and naturally in our lives. All we have to do to prove this to ourselves is to observe children in front of the TV set cheering on the loquacious and innately clever mice as they outwit the clumsy, rodently-challenged cat! And while young children may not be said to be suspending their disbelief willingly, their later behaviour as teenagers while watching movies replete with aliens, axe-wielding zombies and polymorphous blobs indicates that most of us are quite capable of adjusting our belief roster, at least until the movie ends. Similarly, sophisticated patrons at a production of *Hamlet* accept the ghost and his tragic shenanigans for the sake of the play but afterwards vehemently deny the existence of any such chimera. The willing suspension of disbelief is something we learn to do in infancy, long before we know why or come to appreciate the necessity of art and its unique paean of possibility.

To sum up so far, in the reading model whose theory we are elaborating, we have settled on the following key elements:

- The aesthetic aspect of a poem derives from its roots in the verse rhythm.
- Verse rhythm is a fundamental part of children's language acquisition.
- It is characterized by the metrical line; marked cadence; repetition; consonance; simple rhetorical patterning; playfulness and pleasure in language; and reciprocal confirmation and positive emotion between speaker and listener (parent and child).
- The primary aesthetic qualities of a publicly accessible poem-text are, then, those listed above, raised to the level of art only when accompanied by sophisticated and calculated use of the other elements of verse. These primary qualities are embedded in the apparent content but are actually so integrated with the diction, image and the overall structure that they are said to embody and present the meaning (as opposed to expressing or "discoursing" it).
- The verbal-aesthetic structure of a poem-text calls for a reader who is aware of such qualities and purpose, and believes that such a text will yield, in the re-enactment of it, a poem whose meaning is unique and particular, a feeling-thought conveyed in real time.
- The poem's primary aesthetic thus posits a reader who will willingly suspend disbelief until a more analytical or self-conscious rereading is appropriate, and even then the tacit sense of some whole meaning, elusive truth or gestalt insight (the vibrant "myth alive" under and between the words) remains paramount, and one towards which a more focussed reading of parts is always directed.

Before moving on to any pedagogical theory that might be suggested by this paradigm of aesthetic text and reader, we ought to look at two further frequently-occurring features of poems: metaphor and ambiguity. Certainly English teachers will be wondering at metaphor's having been overlooked thus far, as so much of poetry and the discussion of it in class centres on metaphor. In addition, a substantial part of the teacher's time is spent contending with disputatious students over maddeningly ambiguous passages of poetic text.

Metaphor deserves all the attention we lavish upon it. However, even though most poems are awash in it — and in its cousin tropes which include simile, personification, metonymy, allegory, symbol — metaphor remains a secondary aspect of poetry, for its use goes well beyond the bounds of poetry and literature. For instance, various forms of metaphor can be found in expository and argumentative essays, in sermons and editorials, even in the speeches of Hansard, not to mention everyday speech. As a universal comparative device, metaphor is a cogent way of making meaning, and can never be exclusively appropriated by poetry. Conversely, the deployment of genuine poetry in discursive settings is limited (a pithy quote from the Bard, an illustrative couplet from Bartlett) and usually spotted as a device pressed into service from another, and more exotic, sphere. In brief, it is not metaphor that makes poetry poetry.

Nonetheless, when used in poetry, metaphor is no longer an ordinary, adventitious comparative trope; instead, it becomes part of the whole, and is governed and qualified by its aesthetic context: rhythm, sound, line and phrase structure, neighbouring images, and so on. The temptation to seize on metaphor as a shorthand way of translating the meaning of a poem, to get at "thought" quickly and efficiently, will have important implications for teaching. By thinking of metaphor as a secondary trait, we might better keep our initial focus on the primary ones.

Having said this, I hesitate to add that there is a deeper sense in which metaphor might be considered a primary trait. If I do so, however, we might get a better handle on ambiguity. There are powerful poems in our language in which there appears to be no obvious metaphoric language (many of Blake's songs, for example), and yet, for reasons not always clear, we choose to see them symbolically or metaphorically.[15] It is as if we come to poetry expecting metaphor of some kind, even in the absence of rhetorical cues or contextual invitations to do so. Why should this be? Are we merely "reading into" the poem, as many of our students indignantly claim?[16] As we shall see in chapter 4, when writers of any age or experience compose authentic poems, they are projecting a feeling-thought *from* themselves *into* the words of the poem, where it takes on verbal-aesthetic contours and crystallizes as a public text.[17] I will make much of the notion of projection later on, as it is a critical concept in compositional theory and the teaching of writing, but I raise it here to suggest, however tenuously, the proposition that when poets project their feelings into the crucible of words-as-poem, they are knowingly letting those poem-words "stand in place of" the original feeling, even though, as many poets have eloquently testified, they realize that their artifice can never fully represent it. In this limited but interesting sense, then, even when it shows no obvious metaphor, every poem is a form of metonymy (the use of the name of one thing to stand for a characteristic of another).

How does this notion lead us to ambiguity? If a poem can only partially and inadequately embody the thought that originally propelled it into being, then surely these partial inadequacies, being frozen as text, ought to hold still long enough for readers to agree on what is being said. Not so, as any grade-twelve class adrift in the surreal dream fantasies of a Gwendolyn MacEwen poem will tell you. They are more than eager to have explained how a poem can render a precise feeling-thought when no two classmates ever seem to agree on its meaning or the emotions it raises in them. The answer here is straightforward, though pedagogically cantankerous: poems are both precise and inherently ambiguous.

Precision is a product of the effort put into a poem's composition; that effort is intentional and is visible whenever we study the working drafts of poets. Because aesthetic readers understand that the poet strove for precision (revising to get the rhythm, sounds and images just right), they agree to read the poem in the same spirit. That many poems fail to be precise (it is noteworthy that we use this as a criterion in judging poetry) or have vague passages,[18] or that many readers lack the skill or patience to discover their precision, will bedevil any teaching but ought not to dissuade teachers from their duty. Every poem worth our while is the product of an effort at being exact, even though students may fail to agree on the result. What they will need to see, over time, is that all readings of a text are always approximations of it, just as the text approximated the poet's original feeling-thought.

In addition to the inherent ambiguity of approximate interpretation,[19] there is the deliberate ambiguity in the feeling-thought of certain poems. Much human emotion is charged with ambivalence, contradiction and paradox; not surprisingly, poets — in quest of exactness — seize upon them and present them to us without mitigation. Any precise reading of them will depend wholly upon the depth and subtlety of the life-experience we can bring to the text.

A third type of ambiguity is that intrinsic to connotation and metaphor. The associative or connotative meaning of a word, phrase or image — as opposed to its literal or dictionary meaning — is by its nature suggestive, and in poems it is extended and qualified by the aesthetic context, rendering any unanimous response to it impossible, even when there is consensus about its principal effect. Metaphor is also ambiguous in the very way it is constructed and operates. While connotative language ripples or shimmers throughout the poem, metaphor's double-sided structure means that no two readers will ever interpret it in exactly the same manner. "The moon was a ghostly galleon tossed upon cloudy seas" is not only a famous line from Alfred Noyes' "The Highwayman," but one that demonstrates metaphoric ambiguity. How is the moon like a Spanish warship in a sea of tossing (cloud-like) waves? It is not shaped like a ship nor is it the colour of one. Perhaps it is being "tossed" like a ship on its cloud-waves? If so, what tells us we can safely infer this? It is a "ghostly" ship (mysterious? spooky? pale?), but what else? A "galleon" suggests the grand, imposing, romantic(?), Spanish ship of the line, that a comparison to a sloop or schooner would not. It also alliterates with "ghostly" and the line is composed of drumming dactyls and trochees, as is the stanza itself. The wind and "torrent of darkness" from the preceding line will also influence our picturing of the scene and the moon's place in it. The two parts of any metaphor — the thing and the thing to which it is, in part, compared — always leave open to interpretation just how much of one part is to stand for or be carried over to the other. Interpretation is further aided by consideration of the surrounding context, the connotations of the individual words that constitute the metaphor, and the skein of rhythm and consonance transporting it to our ears. In "The Highwayman," the entire first stanza sets up the romantic locale, the other-worldly atmosphere and the sense of urgency as the dark protagonist rides into view. The galleon metaphor is but one component of this broader, feeling-laden picture, and must be read as such. The ambiguity of interpretation will result partly from the nature of metaphor itself and partly from its context in a particular poem. Fortunately for teachers, most grade-niners are able to sense tacitly and holistically the overall atmosphere of the stanza and many of its inklings after listening to it just once.

We are now able to add ambiguity to the list of aesthetic traits summarized above (pp. 31–32) and, insofar as metaphor — used here to stand for all figures of speech — is itself ambiguous, we may cautiously include it among them also. Like the other primary elements, ambiguity and metaphor call for a particular kind of reader with particular qualities, values and skills. Unlike the kind of teaching which assumes that the interpretive act is a special type of intellectual exercise and only secondarily an affective one, what is being proposed here lets the reader attend to both thought and feeling. I do not believe that the New Critics were wrongheaded in trying to hypothesize an ideal reader and then, as teachers, setting out to persuade the necessary creature into being. As we shall see, any method of teaching poetry must encompass both a valid conception of what a poem is and, *ipso facto*, the kind of reader it begs. New Criticism simply had too narrow a view of what poems are and how they actually work on readers — including four-year-olds chanting "Alligator Pie."

To sum up this section in a single sentence: an aesthetic poem-text, generated deliberately by a person composing it both from and towards some elusive but powerful feeling in the mind, courteously invites a reader to read aesthetically, to bring into play those skills and responses best suited to achieving a satisfactory re-enactment of the text and all its attendant pleasures, not the least of which is the appropriation of something never before spoken, a kind of knowledge to be gained only from fully realized works of art. Any satisfaction, of course, must be that of the reader, not a mentor or examiner or omniscient critic, for only the reader can recast the text into a poem, and cannot do so under duress. The suspension of disbelief — one of the necessary dispositions — must be voluntary; the feeling-thought urged by the text demands at every turn the reader's passionate attention. No one can *tell* such a reader what a text ought to mean or what the poet really intended; if nothing else, the multiple ambiguities of aesthetic texts make such an impertinence absurd.

Moreover, without any extant rules or compulsory social contract, poets compose and readers freely choose to respond, setting up a tacit covenant between them. That this should be so is a source of constant wonder and evidence of some sublime serendipity at work in an otherwise wicked world. But it happens. And the surest test of its validity is a morning spent in a primary-school classroom, where uninstructed, blissfully ingenuous children will chant, declaim, recite, read in chorus, act out and improvise upon texts; or laugh, cheer and cry at the stories read aloud to them. And they will happily and unselfconsciously compose poems of their own. The paradigm of the writer-reader relationship we have drawn up here has been derived not so much from a study of erudite tracts or the behaviour of mature readers as it has from the performance of children inundated by aesthetic circumstance, and dancing their delight.

Some Pedagogical Principles

We now have the poem and the reader-of-poetry in symbiotic relationship. Here, then, is the starting-point for thinking about what general principles ought to guide teachers of poetry in quest of specific lessons suited to the age and experience of students. If, however, poem-text and reader are grappled together in mutual interdependence, how can we possibly posit the notion of some third party intervening, however tactfully or obliquely? Surely we have argued our way to the conclusion that any intervention is more likely to be disastrous than helpful. Consider, for instance, the insistence on the reader's voluntary suspension of disbelief: most sixteen-year-olds I have taught find it well nigh impossible to set aside their own skepticism or let their often desperate ego needs subside in temporary favour of a poem's intrusions. Furthermore, readers ought to be able to *choose* to adopt an aesthetic-reading posture. But schools are traditionally places where teachers select most of the texts. If we let students do most of the selecting, how can we be sure they will do so for reasons that include any sense of the aesthetic?

At this point we need to step back for a moment and catch our breath. Teachers naturally tend to leap ahead to the practical implications of an issue, as they are what matter in the long run (and the short run, too). But we cannot teach, assist, or catalyze the process of aesthetic reading by *ignoring* the nature of the poem and the kind of reader it demands. Nevertheless, if we can suspend our own disbelief for a while and approach the matter — how to teach poetry — at a level of generality above specific classroom settings and needs, we may be able to deduce some operating principles that are both valid and susceptible to reformulation at levels where they will yield practical advice on how to organize a curriculum, a course of study, or a unit, and even inspire day-to-day lesson planning.

First of all, because a poem is primarily an aesthetic text and as such invites readers to engage it actively and eventually produce an approximation of the poet's original feeling-thought for themselves, we can assume, even before we decide on the efficacy of intervention *per se*, that *any English or language arts teacher must have a full understanding of the process of aesthetic reading, gleaned from dedicated practice.* Here is principle number one: seemingly self-evident. Perhaps, but if we accept it as a *necessary* governing principle for any teacher at any grade level, then we commit ourselves to making certain that aesthetic reading is not ever placed in the care of an adult who does not appreciate poetry, does not read it outside the classroom, or treats it in the presence of students in any way as if it were not primarily aesthetic. Dozens of teachers I have known would be instantly defrocked under such a decree. Yet how can we proceed further without acknowledging such a first principle? Theme-hunting, gradgrinding petal-pullers — however diligent or pupil-friendly — cannot by definition assist students in re-enacting poems out of aesthetic texts.

Assuming that our first principle has been met, we need to discover how a teacher who understands poetry can, in general, encourage students to practise and improve their reading of poems. I have described a process in which the reader voluntarily postpones premature analysis or application of personal experience and idiosyncratic association in order that the text's primary aesthetic manifestations are able to make an indelible first impression. This prompts the deployment of the reader's tacit awareness and understanding, which in turn ought to facilitate response to the parts-whole phenomenon latent in the text. There appears to be room at this early stage of the student-reader's encounter with the poem-text for a teacher to use a variety of strategies designed to ensure an appropriate first reading. Our second pedagogical principle, then, might be stated thus: *teachers will make certain that a student's initial encounters with a poem-text emphasize its essential aesthetic qualities, encourage the kind of reading manoeuvres suited to such a first engagement, and do so without placing themselves between the text and the student.*

Because a reader's initial engagement is crucial to a full and satisfactory response, it follows that the more compatible the match between the text and the reader's interests and experience, the greater will be the probability of an attentive, gripping first encounter. Whether teachers are dealing with naive readers in grade five or maturing ones in grade twelve, the importance of providing them with poems that are suited to both the level of their rhetorical competence and their life experience cannot be overestimated. A poem must present itself to young readers in its most dazzling aesthetic garb and, beyond that first impression, ought to have the capacity to maintain its grip, to repay repeated engagement and, where apt, a closer reading, analysis and extension. Here, then, is a third pedagogical principle: *teachers should provide students with those poems most likely to engender powerful aesthetic engagement and ongoing aesthetic attention.*

But have we not just contradicted our own theory: that the relationship of poem-text-reader is too interdependent to tolerate third-party intervention? Or that the reader must *choose* to respond and re-enact the text as a poem? Not so, at least not yet. It is precisely because an initial and continuing aesthetic engagement is necessary — not only to the reading of an individual poem but to learning how to grow as a reader — that teaching must involve to some degree the provision of texts most likely to do the job. As we shall see, texts can be provided to students in a variety of ways beyond listing them on a printed syllabus. In fact, provision is a more accurate term here than selection because it implies a way of choosing and orchestrating texts that will be educationally nurturant.

Finally, even when teachers not students, choose texts for whole-class study, it is the *way* in which students respond to, and allow themselves to be engaged by, the initial and successive encounters that really matters. Readers must choose whether or not to be engaged by a poem, but that does not mean that they themselves have to choose the poem. The onus is always upon the teacher to make sure that engagement and interest have been achieved.[20] Of course, not all students will be fully engaged by all texts all the time. We are not in pursuit of the perfect pedagogy, but rather a set of consistent, guiding principles that will help us make reasonable decisions.[21] The principle being espoused here is that teachers cannot coerce engagement with text. If teacher-selected texts require such coercion, then the selection was inappropriate and the principle violated.

As mature and sophisticated readers of poetry, teachers are made aware in their daily contact with student-readers of the gap that exists between them. Mature readers seem able to read poems across a wider range of types and in greater depth. But unless we have a clear sense of what "range" and "depth" actually involve, we will be unable to make pedagogical use of something that seems both obvious and significant. As a colleague once told his methods-class (who were momentarily taken aback by his candour), "I want to make my grade-twelve students as good readers as I am."[22] What is it, then, as good readers, that we do? One reason this question is harder to answer than it ought to be is that, because teachers *are* sophisticated and profoundly experienced readers of poetry, by education and disposition, much of the interpretive process they use has become unconscious. For example, on a single reading of a poem, an English teacher is likely to have grasped, tacitly or consciously, aspects of its meaning that an accomplished grade-twelve class would require five or six readings to equal (they would have to be skilled, of course, even to get near it on the sixth go-round).[23] It behooves us, then, to know as much about the aesthetic-reading process and its phases as we can in order, somehow, to assist students to replicate those elements of the process they are able to undertake.

Put another way, after teachers have provided students with a likely text and arranged for the initial encounter or two to be aesthetic, what do they do next, if anything? Well, because they themselves presumably know that there are subsequent kinds of interpretive moves that they could (and do) make — even though many of these have become automatic — they ought to find the means of describing such moves to themselves, and pursuing ways of inducing students to emulate them. This is not news, as almost all of the published handbooks on teaching literature over the past fifty years are replete with advice and examples. The staple technique for what I will call "second reading" — that is, any more studied look at the text after initial encounters and impressions have been completed — is the teacher-initiated question. I have written extensively on both the theory and use of questions in the English classroom,[24] and will not try to summarize that work here, except to make the point that most questions provided to teachers in guides and cribs aim to have students reread or analyze a text with a view to replicating and practising some interpretive technique, either explicitly (for example, "Find three similes, explain their meaning, and show how they assist us in understanding the poem's main theme") or implicitly ("What kind of man is Browning's Duke in 'My Last Duchess'? Look carefully at lines 1-10"). Many such teacher-questions not only do not encourage appropriate rereading, they sabotage it.[25] In short, even though we may, under the first three principles above, devise ways to ensure an aesthetically-apt first reading, we know there is more that can be done, for we ourselves became proficient readers of poetry not only by reading it independently, but also under the guidance and inspiration of one or two excellent teachers who recited it dramatically, interrogated it aloud, organized productive units, and so on. And there were also those university professors who demonstrated their own interpretive processes at lectern and blackboard.[26]

Somehow, then, and where it is likely to be educationally nurturant, we will set in motion some kind of second reading, and part of it will involve some means of interrogating the text. There will be questions, however posed, and their purpose will be to demonstrate interpretive moves that eventually will become so automatic they will form part of the tacit awareness that mature readers possess and use on the *first* reading. (See chapter 3, p. 82 for a description of how this growth occurs.) What a theory of the poem as aesthetic text can help us do is formulate questions, and strategies for using them, that are consistent with the nature of the poem-text and the complex blend of conscious and tacit processing required to cope with its parts-whole way of meaning. This has been the main pedagogical challenge of the past twenty-five years, ever since the decline of New Criticism and the rise of the reader-centred response-to-literature movement.[27] A fourth principle can now be proposed: *where second reading is deemed appropriate, the teacher will design questions and demonstrate interpretive tasks consistent with the aesthetic first reading.*

This principle requires further explanation before we are ready to use it to generate specific ideas for the classroom. The reason for this is simple: too much inappropriate teaching occurs in well-meant but blundering attempts to guide students through a poem using the Socratic method, line by tortuous line or stanza by gruelling stanza. It is not, I hasten to add, the Socratic method itself that is at fault, for it plays a valuable role in second reading. I make this point in the face of two decades of criticism of this method from New Left pedagogues and advocates of Whole Language and Writing Process.[28] Most of their criticism has focussed on *any* sort of direct teacher intervention in the learning process: questions *per se* are permitted, but only so long as the *students* raise them. But this is problematic in itself. For example, will students, despite the fact that they acquired their mother tongue by being immersed in the aesthetic, affective and playful features of language, be able to ask questions that will take them deeper into the meaning of a sophisticated poem and hence further into its unique feeling-thought and all the associative reverberations it may stir in the individual reader?[29] Not necessarily, and, even if they somehow manage to, how will the teacher know? If they can't, what will she do then? The only pedagogically significant point in all of this is, do questions raised by the teacher out of the text actually assist students to read and enjoy the poem, while simultaneously serving as models for them of more advanced interpretive moves that can eventually be absorbed and generalized? If the answer is yes, then teacher-initiated questions are not merely useful but requisite. We need to keep in mind that any student engaged in making meaning out of a poem-text is automatically raising questions of his or her own because that is what all readers do; that is what comprehending is. The teacher's task at any level is to nudge further helpful questions into view.

One of the reasons why so many of our efforts to use questions to direct students back through a text are unsuccessful is related to the notion of the aesthetic in our theory. Poetry is a non-discursive presentational form of expression. But, alas, it comes with the seductive trappings of ordinary discourse; that is, it has an apparent literal meaning stated in grammatical English. Modern poetry in particular eschews an ornate poetic diction and relies more on phrase-structure than the metrical line; hence, it often gives the appearance of ordinary speech: there are recognizable words and sometimes a narrative flow or set-piece description not unlike that in a novel or travel brochure. And because poems are thought to have themes, the temptation to treat the text as if it can be worked through word by word and chunk by chunk until that theme emerges (like the point at the end of an argumentative essay) is often irresistible. By the same token, teachers know that poems *do* have a literal, denotative aspect that cannot be ignored and ought to be impressed upon the reader fairly early in any reading of the text.[30]

Rightly so. But such literal meanings are embedded in, and are as much a part of, the poem-text's *aesthetic* makeup as the rhythm or sound effects. Any attempt to treat the so-called literal level of a poem (for example, doing a plot summary of events in "My Last Duchess") independently of its context suggests to students that the aesthetic qualities and imperative are mere decoration. And if a powerful presentation *has* been used on first reading (say, a recording of Browning's poem read dramatically) with initial impressions recorded (in journals or jottings or oral discussion), certain phrases, events and climactic sections will have necessarily been highlighted simply because an effective poem-text has already been shaped to our ear, to our sense of drama, and to our capacity for visualization. Indeed by now the poem is no longer linear or even chronological. In "My Last Duchess," for example, the story is still present as a narrative, but sudden turns, the abrupt command of the Duke, the unexplained omission of the interlocutor's replies, the descriptive power of the portrait's detail, the tone and tight rhymes, all produce in us a *highlighted* narrative full of initially unanswered questions and the beginnings of bias towards the principal character. Surely second reading must start with *some* acknowledgement of this indelible first impression.

On the other hand, if we merely guide students, on second reading, back through the text from beginning to end in the hope that a closer study of individual words, phrases or tricky tropes will illuminate hidden meanings, we will not only model for students a laborious and inefficient and non-aesthetic pseudo-discursive process, but create a puzzling disjunction between initial encounter and focussed re-engagement. In brief, if the first and second readings are not connected to one another, what are we doing with them? For many teachers, the response here is, often, to pay lip service to first reading and, especially with high-school classes, to get on with the real job of comprehending all the parts and whatever whole can be stitched together out of them. Our fourth principle, then, may present us with the most severe pedagogical challenge because it is both demanding (calling for apparently analytic work in an aesthetic context) and historically troubled: we haven't done well in past endeavours to model readings subsequent to the initial one. Thus have we been prone to justifiable criticism from competing but equally inadequate pedagogies.

The risk during second reading is that, even when the poem-text's parts have been re-engaged aesthetically for the right reasons, the result will still be somewhat fragmented: it will be hard to hold the impression of first reading indefinitely in mind while some form of analysis takes place. In our earlier description of the aesthetic reading process, the reader's satisfactions at the end of first reading include a sense of aesthetic closure, as if we have been watching a painting being composed before us as we wait for the final stroke to be added so that the whole picture might leap out at us, as well as some gestalt glimpse into the feeling-thought radiating from it. A second reading that enhances, deepens and intensifies the original burst of meaning should be capped off, then, by a rereading of the whole text in some fashion so that students can begin to feel just how much of their analysis can be left tacit as they enjoy a final deep reading. In a way, such a re-engagement is really a third reading, a putting-the-pieces-back-together to make certain that the sum of them is seen and felt.

But what do teachers and mature readers do in the world outside school when they themselves have fully read a poem? When they have, as it were, closed the book on it? If the poem has particularly moved us, we often carry it about in our heads for a while; we retain aesthetic and mnemonic passages or an inerasable impression of something grasped whole for the first time. This may lie latent until something in our everyday life or our reading jolts it awake, and fresh associations flow in and out of it. A character like Browning's Duke of Ferrara can become a template of motive and morality that we consciously or unconsciously apply to actual situations in our lives "So-and-so tries to control his wife like the Duke did his Duchess!" Thus the special knowledge we derive from profound immersion in works of art and their effects is extended, and used in a variety of ways in the world beyond. That is to say, we rarely read a poem or novel or see a Shakespearean play only for the immediate pleasure and insight offered. We go to literature expecting reverberations into our own values and feelings and, further on, into our continuing social and ethical lives. Poems are not written merely to provide aesthetic jolts for titillation, instant gratification, and then dismissal.

If poems have an afterlife, then, we ought to consider ways in which we can encourage young readers to extend their aesthetic experience beyond that final reassembling at the end of second reading. This entails finding means of taking the poem (not unaesthetic bits of it like the one-sentence theme) out to other venues, particularly to other poems and works of literature as well as appropriate areas of the students' lives. From this imperative we derive a fifth principle: *teachers will, where apt and productive, encourage students to extend their initial experience of a poem into their personal and social lives and to other literary works, and thus set up a kind of third reading.*

Under this principle, the terms apt and productive serve as more than cursory caveats. Much unintentional harm has been done by teachers who have attempted to keep kids interested in, or to demonstrate the relevance of, poetry by tying together theme-bits from one poem to another, or using parts of a poem to excite class discussion of certain emotions or ideas or ethical questions. (Mary's class, for example, might have been prodded, after a brief excursion through "The Word," to discuss why public school "Christmas" concerts don't feature the traditional carols any more, or whether the poet is really a Christian since Christ was unique and not Everychild, etc.) For third-reading activities involving the comparison of two or more poems to be productive, the following conditions must be strictly met. The initiating text must have been read aesthetically; the text(s) it is compared with or set against must also be read aesthetically either before or during the comparative study. When two or more poems are studied together, the ongoing comparative work should deepen the understanding of each as poems with feeling-thoughts — not as mere containers for themes or devices. When discussion of a poem is extended into the area of personal response (e.g., in journals) or sociological application (e.g., in group discussion), it should have been aesthetically experienced, and part or all of that experience used as prompt or lead-in. Finally, when aesthetic transpositions are used for extension (see chapter 4), the initiating poem should have been fully and aesthetically read, and the recasting in other form (student's poem, dramatized scene, playscript, illustration) should be governed by the feeling-thought experienced initially, not merely by the poem's topic, theme or subject-matter. Teachers should avoid exercises such as "Write another poem about 'spring'."

For most of the time in English classes, then, teachers will work diligently to provide powerful poems appropriate to the age, interests, and reading experience of their students; to set up unconstrained initial encounters where aesthetic text and individual reader can freely meet; to orchestrate with apt questions and tasks a more focussed re-engagement; to revisit the whole poem and, in a sort of third reading, extend the poem's feeling-thought outward in a variety of ways. In addition, although limited to a select group of advanced senior classes (grade twelve, gifted), there is a legitimate place for what might be termed fourth reading.[31]

One of the implications of a theory of the poem as aesthetic text is that it is readers who ultimately choose to recognize the aesthetic nature of a poem and agree to adjust the reading process accordingly. The corollary of these decisions is that readers may also choose to read a poem-text non-aesthetically. Martin, in chapter 1, did not choose to read the assigned poem non-aesthetically: he simply knew no other way of reading. But readers who *can* read aesthetically do not *have* to do so. As Louise Rosenblatt has pointed out, mature readers can go to a poem for either aesthetic or "efferent" reasons.[32] In other words it is the motive that matters. She uses the term efferent to describe any non-aesthetic purpose for reading a poem (or novel or play) or, more positively, any purpose that involves having the text *do* something *for* the reader *in* the world, besides being and meaning aesthetically. Examples abound. Graduate students comb through Margaret Atwood's poetry hunting down animal imagery or categories of victimization. Scholars cull Shakespeare for food imagery, hints of misogyny, Elizabethan world views, Freudian slips. Novels are scanned for sociological import, Jungian archetypes, political incorrectness. Although many such readings are literary in nature, others pay no more than lip service to the aesthetic quality and imperative of the texts under review.

The litmus test is this: if a student or scholar — in studying, say, animal imagery in Atwood — pulls images out of individual poems in order to discuss certain commonalities or their larger symbolic associations or what they reveal about the poet's psyche, then the motive and method is efferent. Even if the images are examined aesthetically within their constituent stanzas and their embedded sound-rhythm (but not the whole poem), the motive and result will still be efferent. This may seem like hairsplitting, but I offer such an example because it illustrates the unique character of aesthetic text and aesthetic reading. In a poem, *every* part qualifies every *other* part and parts include consonance and all the other presentational features of verse. An obsessive use of swine imagery in her oeuvre may imply something about a poet's world view, but each instance of it will mean only what its context in that poem allows. Most graduate students and all seasoned scholars (I hope) know how to read aesthetically and, in most cases, have read the poems they write about whole before they initiate efferent analyses, or fourth reading. There is no question here of good or bad — merely different. But that difference, I maintain, is absolute: aesthetic and efferent are mutually exclusive. For this reason, then, as teachers we must claim and preserve a secure space for the single poem and the aesthetic response it uniquely invites.

Students, of course, are not scholars. Learning to read literature with increasing sophistication and satisfaction should be a continuous and evolving process from kindergarten to the end of high school and beyond. At every level, then, some adequate sanctuary for aesthetic reading (and poetic writing) must be provided. First, second and third readings — as defined above — must be allowed to flourish, wholly and independently. When that has been guaranteed, then and only then, may we begin thinking about exposing students to efferent ways of working with text. Thus a sixth pedagogical principle emerges: *once a teacher is satisfied that the aesthetic nature and effect of a poem have been addressed, where appropriate and without jeopardizing students' right to respond freely to an aesthetic text or confusing them about aesthetic and efferent ways of reading, a variety of fourth-reading activities may be initiated.*

There are two kinds of efferent activity currently in vogue that warrant closer scrutiny. In addition to the ubiquitous theme paper and independent study or project (which can be either third-reading extensions or fragmenting, efferent tasks), we find (1) a mélange of interpretive activities loosely associated with such postmodernisms as feminism and neo-Marxism, where social context and intertextuality are chief concerns and socially-relevant learnings emphasized; and (2) a welter of activities loosely associated with the learn-to-read-by-writing-and-doing school (an offshoot of Writing Process and contemporary progressivism), where novels and poems and even Shakespeare[33] are read by having students *do* self-selected extension work, often on individual stanzas, episodes, chapters or scenes before the whole text has been read (if it ever is). The latter tasks, disguised as third reading "languaging" extensions, are no substitute for the aesthetic processing demanded by first and second reading; without this, they are worthless, and pernicious. We learn to read by reading, not by writing or "deweying." Many other factors may contribute to our success, but they can never be surrogates for the process itself.

Sociological or thematic analysis, however, could well form a legitimate fourth-reading activity, under two conditions. First, the poem, story or novel will have been previously read, absorbed and commented upon as a whole work-of-art, or else simply analyzed in isolation as if it were actually discursive. Second, students will need to be mature enough to understand what they are doing and why.[34] That many English teachers feel uncomfortable with such a procedure is no surprise, as their education and lifelong interests have been broadly aesthetic. Certainly their reluctance must be considered before full-scale units in 'political' reading are imposed on them.

From an examination of what a poem is, of how and why it is composed, the kind of reader it presupposes and invites, and the aesthetic nature of the cognitive reading process set up between text and reader, we have extrapolated six principles to govern English teaching, courses of study, and the overall formulation of a K-to-12 curriculum in aesthetic reading. These are not the only principles we might have deduced, and even these might have been stated otherwise. However, if the general argument so far has been valid, they ought to translate easily into strategies we can use in the classroom.

Implications for Teaching Poetry

Here once again, in abbreviated form, are the six principles. The teacher:

(1) shall understand the process of aesthetic reading and practise it;
(2) shall ensure that the student's first reading of a poem enhances its aesthetic effects and that such an encounter will be direct and relatively unconstrained;
(3) shall provide students with those poems most likely to engender powerful engagement and ongoing aesthetic attention;
(4) shall decide if a second reading is warranted and, if so, design tasks and questions that enhance interpretation and maintain aesthetic integrity;
(5) shall, as a third reading, encourage students to extend initial aesthetic reading(s) of a poem by relating it to personal and social experience, and by transposing it in related aesthetic forms;
(6) shall, after a full aesthetic reading of a poem, where warranted, initiate fourth-reading analyses of it without jeopardizing the student's right to respond or confusing aesthetic and efferent ways of working with text.

General implications

Understanding these principles and the premises that underpin them should enable us to do two important things. First, it should provide a framework of criteria for assessing the suitability of current teaching practice, whatever the grade level. Secondly, it should facilitate the vetting and use of methods and objectives being offered in the professional and official literature: handbooks, courses of study, government guidelines, and theory books. For example, we may need to scrutinize our extension activities in the light of principle (3) above, for there has been a slow drift in many jurisdictions to a more practical and socially relevant kind of English in schools, so that aesthetic texts (still usually mandated) are used as springboards for theme work, personal writing, or languaging with scant attention paid to their formal elements or their aesthetic extension. Theme work can productively emerge from third or even fourth reading, but that assumes *a priori* that first and second reading have been accomplished. Theme work can also emerge nicely from other non-aesthetic aspects of an English course — as part of an independent project, for example — or as the language component of an integrated English and social studies unit. Providing sanctuary for the aesthetic does not imply that English should deal exclusively with imaginative literature and aesthetic reading. As events of the past forty years have proven, English programmes are flexible and open to a wide range of approaches. However, as principles (1) to (4) remind us, a great deal of tacit aesthetic knowledge is brought to the classroom from kindergarten onward, and thus offers teachers a ready-made source that they can tap to shape early reading and writing experiences, and one that, if nurtured, students can continue to draw upon for the next twelve years.

Also, the last few decades have witnessed, for a variety of reasons, a slow but steady erosion in the authority of the teacher, in the efficacy of teacher-directed lessons, and in the necessity of teachers' selecting and orchestrating age-and grade-appropriate reading materials.[35] Even in high school where the set syllabus has maintained its traditional status, the passion for independent study,[36] whatever its intrinsic virtues, has undermined our faith in the vital role that teachers must play if K-to-12 schooling is to provide students with a rational, developmental programme in English. Because aesthetic reading and poetic writing are fundamental linguistic processes learned at the same time as, and intricately bound up with, the acquisition of speech, they are *ipso facto* requirements, not options, in the development of literacy, particularly in the primary grades where there are few, if any, viable alternatives. And while children in these classes show a ready propensity to respond to and produce aesthetic texts and representations (in drama and art), a teacher will be needed to ensure that psychologically compelling stories, poems, myths, legends and fairy tales[37] are available and, equally important, are presented to children in a richly aesthetic environment. This in turn means that teachers should know how to select such materials and organize lively lessons around them. By the same token, much of the faddish student-centred, student-governed pedagogy will have to be vetted, and most likely abandoned.

In the other grades, the six principles pointedly advise that the self-selection of novels and poems by students cannot be a major aspect of an English course because the likelihood of students' responding to them aesthetically on first reading is reduced or uncertain, for the texts chosen, while aesthetic, may not be rhetorically powerful enough to engage readers in ways that promote growth and develop new skills. Middle-school students will need both Judy Blume and *The Secret Garden*.[38] Furthermore, unless the teacher is knowledgeable enough to set specific questions for each student-selected text, no opportunity will be presented to engage students in second reading or appropriate extension activities. Generic tasks and all-purpose assignments will have to go — at least in that part of English that purports to deal with literature and poetic writing.

On the other hand, the role of the teacher as master-instructor, as sole selector of texts from the received canon, as expert validator of student responses and final arbiter of interpretation, this kind of authority (popular before the social revolution of the sixties and now threatening to retake the dais), is incompatible with the aesthetic-reading process and the demands of aesthetic-based second and third reading. In particular, many such teachers were (and are) incapable of keeping their interventions from disturbing the student's critical first encounter with the text, and their second-reading questions are invariably overly analytical ("Let's begin with a close look at the image in line 1") or haplessly vague ("What is the poet trying to say here?"). The danger that we face at the beginning of the twenty-first century is that the fifteen-year flirtation with the soft pedagogies of the student-centred movement[39] will give way to a pendulum-swing back to the good old days, in tandem with the current neo-conservative political agenda. Only a sound theory of how reading happens and a matching set of incontrovertible pedagogical principles has any hope of stabilizing literacy teaching.

What the argument I have been making thus far (and we still have poetic writing to consider) has been pointing to is that aesthetic texts do exist as definable, describable entities. They have, as Steiner has insisted, "real presence." Poets compose freely and readers seek them out independently. And because the crafted feeling-thought of poems has the potential to engage the feelings and thoughts of the passionately attentive reader — even when tacit or perhaps even subliminal — the content or message is neither vague nor insignificant. It is easy to see why neo-Marxists, feminists, and anti-racist groups — among others — have not only viewed literary works in the same discursive-ideological light as political tracts, magazine articles or television commercials, but also considered them to be potentially more insidious because their aesthetic impact subverts the intellect and its skeptical antenna.[40] (Plato came to much the same conclusion, and banished poets from his republic.) Moreover, if the so-called message is indeed a constituent part of the meaning of a poem, thereby rendering it subversive by nature, then there seems little point in bothering to include a roster of powerful (and dangerous) works of literature in K-to-12 English. Surely a few weeks each year in social studies or in the propaganda unit of a practical English programme could be devoted to the active analysis of selected literary texts. In other words, why bother teaching kids how to respond to the aesthetic qualities in literature when these are seen primarily as instruments of propaganda akin to a TV jingle for hand soap or the sentimental music in a romantic movie? Indeed, the unresolvable, internecine controversies in recent years over *whose* propaganda to include in the choice of novels for English courses would seem to suggest the futility of the exercise, whatever the approach.

There is more. Despite the temptation to single out ideologically offensive bits (a predilection that has exacerbated the controversy over text selection), it is the *full* meaning of a poem or novel that must be used as the basis for any debate about its suitability, not some premature and wrong-headed targeting of politically incorrect parts. If a poem is judged to be generally offensive or inappropriate for a certain age or group, it needs to be deemed so in light of its probable effect as a uniquely crafted feeling-thought. In brief, the aesthetic impact of the whole poem, engendered by a teacher-guided aesthetic reading, is what needs to be discussed before the text is banished or embraced.[41] Literary works are not harmless: they reverberate with meaning and, as we have seen, that meaning, in an aesthetically charged environment, is likely to be open-ended and variable. Ambiguity is a given, and any closure is going to be temporary and consensual, not finite and singular.

In this sense, poems and novels are even more hazardous than many critics think. It is not the intertextual niceties of the poem that are likely to insinuate the vulnerable defenses of the young, but rather the upfront dithyrambics and image dazzle, the sudden and ineradicable contours of a metaphor, or its infinite emotional resonance. In sum, literature ought to be included in English studies for what it is or, if that is not acceptable, simply struck from the syllabus. The other goals often associated with literature (especially in government prescriptions for the senior grades), such as, its contribution to knowledge about the past, to our multicultural heritage, and to the expansion of thought, language and rhetoric, these could surely be addressed by suitable non-aesthetic or discursive texts or by sociological novels too literal and artistically pallid to be subversively ambiguous. Put another way, the foregoing argument underlines the necessity of our abandoning specious claims for the dominant place

Aesthetic Reading: Poetry 49

still accorded classic literature in grades seven to twelve: in a quixotic effort to save it from the philistine hordes at the gates. If it is to serve principally as fodder for anti-aesthetic street-proofing, as cultural content (politically corrected), or as textual *matériel* for stretching vocabulary, then any pretense to treating it aesthetically must be dropped.

If literature is to be dealt with as essentially aesthetic — and I do believe it has a necessary place in the K-to-12 curriculum — it will have to be handled by teachers who know this and are prepared to use the knowledge for educational ends, both despite and because of the risks entailed. In general, they will have to have the expertise, sensibility and conviction to prompt aesthetic responses, and to honour them and their ambiguities. They will be prepared to choose texts, devise sequenced reading tasks, compel with exquisite tact[42] aesthetic engagements and extensions, and lead students to a progressively clear understanding of literary and discursive texts, and how they work in the world.

Kindergarten to Grade Three

An understanding of the process of aesthetic reading, principle (1), leads to some very specific conclusions about teaching English or the language arts in the primary grades. Any explicit form of second reading is bound to be unproductive, for although students *can* give answers to questions about form and content, they are not yet self-conscious enough as cognitive processors for such tasks to be internalized, rendered automatic, and tacitly deployed. Hence, the latter are destined to be "overlearned" as a discrete way of working with text outside the governance of any first-reading impression. In Kieran Egan's useful term, this kind of learning is "inert," as opposed to being an "aliment" (that is, educationally nurturant and capable of stimulating further growth).[43] So, most teaching manuals attached to reading anthologies or series — replete with quizzes and exercises — will have to be jettisoned or carefully screened to ensure that any reflective second reading comes only after a full engagement, and then only indirectly. For example, "Listen to the description [in *Charlotte's Web*] of Charlotte, the spider, catching a fly, as I read it again, and tell me how you think Wilbur feels about her." Indeed, since principles (1) to (3) ought to dominate teaching in the reading programme in these grades, *immersion* in aesthetic texts in an aesthetic atmosphere will be the governing criterion.

The seminal work of Don Holdaway[44] demonstrates the role of story and poem in preschool language acquisition — including internalized syntax, story- and poem-grammar — and the efficacy for stimulating early reading of teacher-orchestrated lessons centred on poetry. In *The Foundations of Literacy* he lays out both a learning theory and an exemplary pedagogy for the primary school literacy curriculum, with emphasis upon automaticity and tacit knowledge. Besides using literary texts to teach students to decode print (including contextualized phonics), Holdaway is *at the same time* expanding the store of tacit knowledge that emergent readers will need to become proficient readers of more complex aesthetic texts and, by extension and later on, discursive ones as well. By the same token, reading discursive texts of any true complexity must be delayed, despite the pressure on schools to be practical and real, simply because there is so little tacit foundation for inexperienced readers to draw on. Most students below grade eleven or so do not read essay-like texts extensively out of class, as they do novels, nor has their preschool linguistic experience funded a store of syntactical and rhetorical models for the elaborated sentence and the discursive paragraph, as it has for verse and poetry.

Immersion, then, will form the basis for methodology in primary school. Which means engagement, re-engagement (what Holdaway terms revisiting old favourites), and extension through transpositional activities: poem read transposed to drama, illustration or student's poem. In *Stability and Change in Literacy Learning*, Holdaway provides two detailed lesson sequences, one for emergent literacy and one for early reading, that should serve as models for an aesthetic-based classroom (see resource section below). Dramatic activities, choral reading, corporate response, poetic writing of all kinds, these will be the staple fare. And by grade three or four a gradually expanding independent-reading component will be added to facilitate out-of-class reinforcement and the acquisition of more tacit knowledge, which will be foundational to learning several grades onward. It is paradoxical but true that much of the consequence of effective teaching in an aesthetically oriented classroom will not be manifested (or be measurable) in the immediate school year, making it difficult for authorities to establish clear accountability or neatly graduated standards of achievement. But if the learning paradigm that underpins the teaching principles here is valid, all they need to do is make certain that nurturing, long-term, supportive activities are encouraged and recorded.

Conversely, the six principles permit us to critique and assess other pedagogies competing for attention. For example, the popularity of Ken Goodman's *What's Whole in Whole Language?* and the many practical guides and materials it has spawned can be countermanded by a cold appraisal, one that finds Whole Language theory and suggested practice to be unaesthetic, even, at the extreme, antiaesthetic. To wit: Goodman lists reading literature as merely one among five pragmatic functions of print (not language), its purpose being "recreational."[45] Novels are lumped in with hobby books and other leisure-time reading. The suggested pedagogy for Whole Language supports this truncated view of aesthetic texts: student choice of books is valorized and the teacher's role correspondingly shrunk to that of facilitating observer (or "kid watcher"). While it may be true that such flawed, student-oriented pedagogy will in fact promote collaboration and social cohesion, and even encourage kids to seek out books and read them, the absence of aesthetic strategies to enhance engagement and meaningful extension, and activate internalized capacities could prove fatal. For the risk is too great that many children will not learn to read in ways that consolidate what they already tacitly know and that provide a basis for future efficiencies and competencies. As a sociolinguistically-driven theory of learning to read, Whole Language has always been an incomplete pedagogy. Many of its highly touted ancillary benefits — teachers who listen, students adept at group discussion, supportive schema for independent reading, the writing workshop — never were intrinsic or exclusive to the Whole Language approach, and therefore should not be raised spuriously in its defense. As a major methodology for teaching literacy in primary school (or elsewhere) it is indefensible.

Grades Four to Nine

The middle years are the most challenging ones for the teacher who wishes to implement an aesthetic-based pedagogy in English. The joys and heady satisfactions of immersion, unalloyed engagement, poetic expression and dramatic enactment that characterize the primary school cannot be indefinitely maintained. Certainly much of the work in poetry in grades four to seven will continue to focus on initial engagement, but it is during these years that most students begin to become conscious of the language and formats that they have been tacitly manipulating since infancy. They soon realize that poems are not short stories, nor do all of them come in the same package or shape. While students prefer to read rhymed poetry, they prefer to write open-form verse.[46] If rhyme is not the hallmark of verse, then what is, they begin to wonder. In short, these students are ready for some initial, tactful reflection: on the "thing" being read, on their own first responses, and on those puzzling parts of a poem previously glossed over by mutual consent. Students of this age also begin to become fully aware of metaphor as a form of deliberate comparison, so that merely responding to the emotional suggestiveness of a given metaphor or to a gestalt-like grasp of its import starts to give way to an intimation (at least) that some reflective reconsideration of it might prove fruitful.

The task for the teacher in these early middle years, and later as well for those students with minimal reading experience and less-developed ability, is to take initial engagements with poetry from first to second reading, principle (4), and to seek other ways of bringing its formal-aesthetic aspects to more conscious attention. The ideal method for doing so is the student-response journal,[47] for it is a vehicle that permits individual students to write down their first reactions quickly, as they listen, or immediately after a poem has been read aloud to them. An effective alternative is to have students jot down quick responses in point form, which, like journal responses, can then be used to prompt a second reading or re-engagement.[48] Because unconstrained first responses will necessarily vary, the teacher can capitalize on the variations to take students back to the text for a second look at selected parts, with lots of oral rereading to maintain the aesthetic context.

The example below indicates four ways in which an initial engagement with a poem can be extended to include some form of second reading. The variants are sequenced from the least analytical to the most. It is up to the judgement of the teacher as to the readiness of students to handle any analysis of parts, with principle (4) as a guide. At the first sign that aesthetic integrity is being compromised — that is, the analysis of parts is overwhelming any sense of the whole achieved on first reading — the teacher should retreat gracefully to some rounding-off activity with the whole text. Reflective reading, the selected re-engagement of parts, cannot be forced or rushed because students, especially advanced readers, may become confused about which game is the real one: those unconstrained, emotionally prompted impressions of the whole text or the careful, seemingly less ambiguous, and certainly more rational examination of manageable parts.

Responding to Poetry

Expressive Writing / Expressive Talk
The teacher announces that she is going to read aloud a short lyric poem and says, "In your response-journals, as soon as I've finished reading, take four or five minutes to write down your immediate response." She reassures students that, as usual, they will not be *required* to read out or otherwise reveal their written responses. (Response-journals are reviewed by the teacher later on at specified intervals.) After the reading, the teacher directs students into their regular groups to "discuss the poem in any way you like. You may refer, directly or indirectly, to your journal entry." (The text may be supplied on paper or overhead, or may be kept back for second reading. Students talk for ten to fifteen minutes. A variation here is to add a single prompt; e.g., "Write down your feelings as you listen to the last line.")

This first reading may constitute the whole lesson (with only the teacher's review of individual journal entries later on), with a new poem the next day. But when second reading is desired, one of the following variations may be chosen. They go from the most open-ended (centred on personal response with the least prompting or intervention) to the most analytical (more closure, consensus, working of parts, teacher guidance).

1. No formal take-up in class, but students are asked to write a second, more reflective journal entry (in class or at home) after the discussion and with the text available for rereading. The teacher will see both entries during periodic review of the journals.
2. The teacher "chairs" a sharing of the thoughts and feelings of each group, with no *directing*. A board summary is optional. Students are asked to write a second, reflective entry at home, preferably on an issue or point raised during the take-up. In a board outline, general headings are helpful to track students' common and individual responses; e.g., Feelings, Reactions, Associations, Content. But the teacher does not redirect towards the text, only other student responses.
3. The teacher takes up group and individual responses, with the text in view, *shaping* and *highlighting* what is said (on the blackboard, as above) and redirecting towards *gaps* in the text or broad areas of response: story, allegory, associa-

> tive aspects, form/rhetoric (where useful to meaning). This is a low-risk, inviting method of introducing second reading: a whole-class, Socratic lesson where analysis is driven by initial, open-ended responses in journals and group talk. The lesson ends with a general consensus and/or a reflective entry in student journals where they sum up their feelings and views. Some poems will lend themselves to a prompt that might focus initial responses and aid subsequent discussion.
> 4. As above (variation 3), but the teacher guides first-responses towards some overriding aspect of the text, provided that initial student responses permit it. A single prompt at the beginning is helpful in setting up the desired aspect, but it must always be open-ended in terms of the reader's feelings. (See chapter 3, pp. 92–93 for examples of such prompts.) The focus here could be a comparison with previously read poems (a unit theme, issue, emotion, genre, motif) or some close analysis: to fill in major gaps in first response or deal with strong ambiguities (no nitpicking!) or to set up a reflective response in students' journals. Although analytical, any re-examination of parts will be driven by first-response and will appear to be in aid of a richer response, not a line-by-line reworking of the text.

Many variations can be worked from this basic model, but there are numerous other ways in which the middle-school teacher can prepare students for the kind of second reading that will be required in the senior grades, where more intricate and ambiguous texts will predominate. Indeed, it is the abrupt switch from immersion techniques or stilted analysis in elementary school to the serious business of really reading poems in high school that explains why so many advanced readers become "poem-o-phobic." We all learn to read particular kinds of texts in stages. Teachers must allow students to inhabit those necessary stages, as *we* did, for as long as they need to. As Kieran Egan has argued, skipping stages in learning is always a mug's game;[49] however, by nurturing and enriching the phase students are already in and comfortable with, we ensure that they will be ready to move on. Put another way, we are always on the watch for Vygotsky's zone of proximal learning.

The practical suggestions in the list below are designed to indicate to teachers that many non-analytical or preanalytical methods exist for judicious use and tactful sequencing. A prior requirement for the successful use of these suggestions is the selection of poems that have a strong initial appeal to students, do not present overly complex rhetorical challenges, and are not too intrinsically ambiguous. My own preferences for the middle-school years are poems with one or more of these features: vivid imagery, narrative or contrastive structure, density of consonance and pronounced rhythm, sustained metaphor or personification, and strong feeling, on topics like love, nature, seasons, animals, children, and old age.

Non-analytic Ways of Teaching Poetry

1. Choral reading:
During or following the class discussion of a poem, key stanzas or lines are read by the boys, then by the girls, with discussion of the effect of deep or light voices on the overall mood. Dramatic poems can be read as parts or roles, with narration and chorus. Many narrative-dramatic poems can be taught in this way: interpretation is worked out "as we go." Groups are asked to prepare an impromptu reading of a poem (before or after a first reading), and then groups read aloud, with comparisons made as to how (and why) certain readings came about. These may be taped for replay. A long poem like "The Highwayman" is read and discussed generally (with focus on the main storyline and principal characters and motive). Time is set aside each day for several days to prepare a polished choral reading involving the whole class, with sound effects, musical background, etc. Sections are read chorally and/or individually, as appropriate. The understanding of the poem deepens during the rehearsal period. Regular discussion groups might be asked to prepare, for the whole class, ideas for presenting a particular stanza or section, and all group ideas pooled. The final reading may be taped as a radio programme, with introduction and music, to be played to other classes. The polished choral reading is reworked in more dramatic form for presentation at an assembly.

2. Presentation:
A poem is discussed in groups without any teacher introduction (alternatively, students might take five minutes to write individual responses in their journals after reading the poem

silently). One student is designated to read it aloud to the whole class, using the interpretative advice supplied by the consensus of the group. The whole class discusses and compares readings. Groups select a series of lyrics from sources supplied by the teacher on a given motif (love, sadness, joy of spring, grandparents, etc.) and prepare an audiotape for presentation to the class. Students choose the best method of presenting the material, including dramatic sequencing, use of chorus or dramatic parts, music, and sound effects. As the tape is played, the other students respond in their journals, with follow-up discussion. Students choose a favourite lyric poem, and present it to the class: reading it aloud several times, and discussing why they chose it and how they went about preparing to present it. Students select, individually or in groups, children's verse, and prepare a presentation for a primary class in the school. (Dennis Lee's collections are sure winners here.)

3. Informal reading and discussion:
The teacher arranges on a single sheet, to be duplicated, five or six short poems related by topic or mood or situation. Some or all of the following activities are then carried out in a relaxed, conversational atmosphere:

The teacher reads one poem (the anchor poem) aloud, and asks students to jot down or make journal-entry responses on the mood, feeling, etc. Responses are discussed, and then a second poem (on the sheet) is read aloud, and students are asked "What do you feel is similar here about the mood (feeling, viewpoint)?" "What seems different?" Students are then asked to read, alone or in groups, the remaining two or three poems and comment on the links (similarities and differences) with the first two. Any group work should be brisk and no longer than ten minutes, as free-wheeling discussion and browsing through the poems is the aim here. Direct prompts can be helpful; e.g., "Spring makes poet A joyful but poet B sad; have you ever had both these reactions?"

Students are put in their groups and asked to browse through the poems on the sheet to see what topic or feeling or issue they may have in common. The general topic (nature, friendship) may be given in advance with an open prompt such as "How many different views or attitudes to nature do you find in these descriptions of spring?" Whole-class discussion ensues with ample rereading and reference to the texts, with a focus on a deepening sense of variations on a theme.

The set of poems is chosen to reflect an ongoing unifying theme, and informal questions are raised about the poets' particular ways of handling the theme, with the whole class or in groups.

4. Other approaches:
The teacher reads aloud a poem related to an immediate issue raised during the study of a novel or unit of stories, and the class, or groups, discuss its relevance to that issue.

The teacher reads aloud, or plays a professional reading of, strongly narrative verse or nonsense verse for pleasure. Students listen or write free responses or take turns reading with the teacher or give their opinions on the genre.

A special weekly time is set aside for poetry appreciation, where students and teacher share favourite poems, take turns reading poems they have selected, discuss favourite authors, types of poetry, song lyrics, etc.

Students are asked to select five or more poems that they like from books supplied by the teacher or librarian. One of several formats may be used: involving illustrations, cover art, an introduction ("Why I chose these poems"), a comment at the end of each poem (which has been written out or typed by the student) about its meaning or appeal, inclusion of one of the student's own poems, and/or supporting photographs or collages. Anthologies may be discussed, passed around for reading, or commented on by the teacher. Group anthologies (on a unit-theme), student-written collections, autobiographies (with a mix of chosen favourites, student compositions, and photographs) are interesting variations.

When students write their own poetry, they get to experience how others respond to it; for example, the teacher in private or their peers during voluntary read-your-own sessions with the class. Many suggestions for stimulating students to write poetry appear in chapter 4.

The middle grades are fertile terrain for poetic writing of all kinds: poem, story (incident), myth, legend, fairy tale, radio play, dramatic scene(s). In composing poems and other poetic texts of their own, students are often surprised to discover that they have externalized much tacit knowledge and skill that they have acquired long before. Opportunities abound for reflecting upon their own productions in the follow-up to writing lessons, as well as during any subsequent revision process. In fact, many third-reading extension activities — often a substitute for more analytical second reading when the latter is inappropriate — also provide an opening for students to see the poetic text as a crafted object or frozen form of art-speech. For the first time they may be looking at the "thing itself."

In the past twenty years or so, the middle grades have been the target of many fully worked out methodologies, with excessive claims to both their efficacy and practicability. To cite just one of the more egregious efforts: Atwell's *In the Middle*,[50] an ambitious and vastly influential programme of English studies for grades seven and eight, is incompatible with a vigorous, aesthetic-based approach to reading and writing. This can be seen in Atwell's emphasis on student choice of text, task, and follow-up activity; on a workshop model that limits the teacher's capacity to *present* poems and stories in engaging ways and as a whole (the ten-minute mini-lesson reigns supreme); on student-formulated criteria for measuring growth in reading competence; and on a weak collateral poetic-writing component (generated from the student's personal experience only). More specifically, there is simply not time or opportunity enough for adequate first reading or much second reading, and, where there is, the latter is not governed by initial aesthetic response or guided by the teacher, who seems to be an odd combination of cheerleader and record keeper. And its theory of how kids learn to read is superficially "environmental" (Piagetian) and relentlessly instrumental: just get them *doing* it and everything else will fall into place! The middle-school years, and poetry, are too important to be left to such earnest but muddled assumptions.

Grades Ten to Twelve

In the senior grades, advanced readers[51] will be introduced to classic poetry from the past and a cross-section of contemporary poems deemed to be culturally valuable and of interest to adolescents. These poems demand second reading and often reward third reading extension, like comparative work in theme and form, as part of an ongoing unit. There will be no need to persuade students to re-examine puzzling parts of, say, Eliot's "Prufrock" after an initial engagement. Unanswered questions will hang visibly before teacher and students, challenging both. This fact is so self-evident that the temptation to pay lip service to a first read-through and get straight to the tough stuff is often irresistible. Nevertheless, a fully engaged and relatively unconstrained first response is not only important here, it is obligatory. If students have, ideally, been guided through the middle-school years with an intelligent melding of engagement, reflection and extension, then both their acquired interpretive skills and their internalized tacit understandings need to be tapped and exercised. It is to be hoped that students will have discovered the interpretive value of their holistic responses, and will have come to trust and deploy them in intensifying and adjusting the poem's meaning during any second look. For the senior teacher to abandon first reading abruptly, or subtly depreciate it, will be confusing and self-defeating. On the other hand, if students have received haphazard and conflictive training in reading poetry in grades five to nine (an all too likely possibility), they will more than ever require an "immersion and engagement" pedagogy to compensate for what they have missed and to be put back in touch with the tacit knowledge they possess but have never been prompted to use. The sample lesson given below has been designed to appeal to both kinds of student. (Also, variations on it have been run from grades seven to twelve.)

It is in the senior grades also that questions of ambiguity in poetry arise almost daily, and refuse to go away. More than ever, teachers will need to shepherd students through these interpretive thickets. Beginning a unit of poetry with the writing of poems under strong stimuli (see chapter 4, pp. 108–109) is often an effective prelude to having students discuss the less-than-conscious way that they — like poets — produce a first draft; that is, the tapping of their tacit knowledge is made visible. And if poets compose, during the first-draft phase, in gestalt-like, holistic leaps where the sound and shape of a phrase is uttered as a unit of feeling-thought, then perhaps readers ought to read such a text in similar spirit. In reading aloud students' own poems during the follow-up to a writing session, the teacher may ask the other students to jot down their responses. In the ensuing general discussion, critical questions are incidentally raised about whether the student-writer "intended" her readers to react in such-and-such a manner and how it is that no two responders captured exactly the same meaning. And so on. The replication with student-produced poems (induced under strong stimuli) of the issues of intention and ambiguity of interpretation is an excellent preparation for the more exacting second reading of poems on the syllabus.

In addition, as a further softening-up exercise, students should be taken through several of the early forms of engagement and immediate response (see items 1. to 3. on p. 108) with fairly complex and ambiguous texts — with a view to getting them used to processing poems at various levels of intensity and completeness. If senior students with better than average linguistic ability are to learn ultimately that the interpretation of poem-texts is always open-ended, the notion needs to be introduced early and then explicitly modelled. That is to say, not every poem studied in class will be rounded off or left at the same stage of completion. Aesthetic texts, as our principles suggest, do not work on us that way. The best that can be achieved in a senior classroom is a group effort at first, second and third reading, with a consensus only about what has been "meant" and absorbed, that is, a sense of how much meaning can be agreed upon as common and how much must be left to each individual reader and to further readings in the future.

Once the teacher is satisfied that students have gained confidence in the legitimacy of their initial response to the aesthetic qualities of poems, a sustained second reading may be introduced. For example, a discussion of students' journal responses or point-form jottings after an initial encounter should yield questions or areas of ambiguity that could well set the framework for reflective analysis and re-engagement. Sometimes a carefully worded question posed by the teacher to open up discussion of a rhetorical pattern or cluster of key images is useful, especially if students are put into their groups for ten to fifteen minutes, followed by a whole-class take-up lesson. For it is on second reading that the ambiguities and special language of poetry will slowly be made explicit. Moreover, because analytical work is required, it is even more important that it be governed by confirmation and refinement of first responses, and that any analysis of parts will be concluded by a rereading of the whole poem and, from time to time, a further journal entry by each student after the event in which they repossess the poem as their own.

An aesthetically sensitive second reading also makes way for a richer and more varied third reading. In this regard, poetry in the senior grades should normally be taught in units of a week or more, with poems grouped by theme and format (love and romance in ballad, sonnet, and contemporary lyric; poems about poetry; poems about war, mortality, etc.) so that productive comparison can be made, not as a gimmick or pseudo-connective, but in order to have students see, for instance, how a feeling-thought has been expressed in varying forms, or how common formats are adjusted to suit particular themes or feelings. It is only by experiencing the continuous, intense study of a number of commonalities and variations within a planned unit that maturing readers can steadily come to grips with the fundamental features of aesthetic text and its purpose. For this to occur, over time, all three phases of aesthetic reading must be brought fully and routinely into play. As mature readers, we never abandon a first response to presented text in favour of close analysis, nor do we jettison close analysis in favour of larger thematic or generic considerations.

Third reading at the senior level, of course, entails the extension of how individual texts are read into a growing understanding of genre, literature and culture, the place of biographical and historical circumstance and poetic composition. The study of successive drafts of a poem from manuscript variants; a focus on Canadian, American, or women poets, etc.; selecting and creating a personal anthology of poems; preparing poems for choral reading or presentation to the class — these are just a few of the third-reading activities that senior students ought to be involved in as they learn more about how aesthetic text works in the world. And with many mature and advanced readers, some tactful introduction to other critical methods might be attempted. However, students must never become so enthralled with generic, cultural and thematic overviews that they lose sight of the primary and root activity: reading a poem with insightful delight.

What follows is a sample lesson on a well-known and much-anthologized poem by e.e. cummings.[52] It is an ambiguous and reverberative text that demands an attentive initial response to its sounds and rhythmic phrasing, and raises genuine questions that only a perceptive rereading can address. While one lesson cannot illustrate all the features of a thoroughgoing aesthetic approach to poetry in grades ten to twelve, the one below is meant to illustrate the way in which the three stages of reading can be integrated to deal with a challenging, subtle, and wonderfully ambiguous masterpiece.

Phase one: Read the poem aloud to the class, while students listen (the text is not supplied at this stage). Then pause and say, "I'm going to read the poem again, and this time I want you to jot down, as you listen or immediately after I finish reading, two or three adjectives to describe the feelings the poem arouses in you." A blank sheet of paper, not a notebook,

in Just-
spring   when the world is mud-
luscious the little
lame balloonman

whistles   far   and wee
and eddieandbill come
running from marbles and
piracies and it's
spring

when the world is puddle-wonderful

the queer
old balloonman whistles
far   and   wee
and bettyandisbel come dancing

from hop-scotch and jump-rope and

it's
spring
and
     the

          goat-footed

balloonMan   whistles
far
and
wee[53]

should be used. Give students about thirty seconds to record their responses after the reading is completed. Go to the blackboard and record, without editorial comment, as many responses as are forthcoming. Group the adjectives, or transpose the non-adjectives, as you go along, then put a heading on the column so that it now looks something like this:

1. Tone / Mood

happy	bouncy
cheerful	light
gay	springy
child-like	fast
fantastic	quick
skipping	
sad	
melancholy?	scary?

Some classes will immediately detect the shift in tone and rhythm when they hear "and / the / goat-footed / balloonMan," while others will detect the sad diminuendo effect of "far and wee" on its third iteration. If there is such a shift of tone evident in these first holistic responses, make note of it in this manner: "Well, most of you found it a happy, bouncy poem, but one or two found it sad, even scary. I wonder why? I'm going to read the poem again, and ..."

Phase two: This time students are asked to write down all the things they see and hear (places, people, actions) in response to the instructions, "Let's find out what makes some of you happy and some sad." Students write as they listen, and are given three or four minutes to complete their jottings. Begin now to map the poem's literal content on the blackboard in a second column beside the first one. The order and grouping of words is not central here; the class should work quickly until all relevant information is before them in some form. Some prompting may be needed to fill gaps with questions, such as, "Did the boys have names? What were they? Are you sure?" "Are these all the words used to describe the balloonman? Is he moving at all?" Some gaps may remain and some questions about what is going on may be left outstanding: leave them as is, for they nudge students to another reading, into pattern, metaphor and symbol. Now link up the first and second responses by referring back to column one: "Which adjectives in this column would express your reaction to 'mud-luscious'? Why? Do we have anything here in column two that might be 'scary'?" The connotations of "little lame" and "queer old" may have triggered the scary or sad note; if not, read the second half of the poem again and ask students to listen for any change in tone or mood. That is, do not hesitate to prompt responses by re-engagement with aesthetic "bits." Prompting is not leading; it is bringing readers and text into aesthetic proximity again. The blackboard may now look something like this:

1. Tone / Mood   2. Content

(as above)   just spring
                      spring
                      mud-luscious
                      puddle-wonderful

                      Eddie and Bill   marbles and piracies
                      Betty and Isobel   hopscotch and jump-
                                            rope
                      Isbel?
                      come running
                      come dancing   to? from?

                      balloonman   whistles
                      little lame   far and wee? whee?
                                            we?
                      queer old
                      goat-footed

Phase three: The content is out and so is the narrative movement, but the contrast or conflict in mood, evident on the initial reading or becoming evident on the second one, is still unexplained. This allows you to set up another engagement, thus: "What words, images, objects do you hear repeated? In what order?" The poem is read aloud again. Students jot down responses. In a third column on the board, begin to reconstruct the details of column two so that the picture now takes into account the placing of objects in space and time. The full power of connotation and metaphor should now be felt, confirming some of the intimations of first response. For example, the connotations of "little lame," "queer old" and "goat-footed" are now examined in the order of their appearance: "Is this the same balloonman? Does he change as we watch? In readers' eyes? In the eyes of the children in the poem? Is he getting closer or farther away?" Prompts like these will draw students into speculation on their own responses, and relevant sections of the poem will be read aloud many times here as the subtleties of tone and image shift are progressively unveiled. The movement from joy and innocence to the sinister undertones of the goat-footed creature leading them — where? — will be aided by the sounds of "mud-luscious" and "puddle-wonderful" (assonance of *u*, onomatopoeia of lus*cious*), but these will be dealt with indirectly: "Do the sounds and images change your feeling about the scene as it unfolds?" Teacher points, prompts and rereads with relish, but only the students can give their responses. There is no right answer, only further pursuit of questions and gaps already evident. In sum, what can be richly explored in this phase is how one image shifts our perspective when set against a repeated pattern, and that by the end of the sequence serious new questions are suggested: did the *children* see the change in the man? Where are they going? Is "far and wee" ultimately a happy or a sinister sound? Why a balloonman and not a popcorn vendor? Why is he *whistling*? In most of the classes where I have used this lesson, at least one student tentatively raises the notion of a Pied Piper or Pan. While hoped for, this insight should be left to the students. With senior classes, one open prompt might be essayed: "Does the balloonman remind you of anyone?"

Meantime, the first two columns remain on the board to provide the class with a record of the ear's initial impressions of tone and mood, and the translation of words heard into visualized objects. Both phases one and two act as a quick check against any tendency to over-allegorize during the crucial third phase. And analysis can now be seen by students to take place under the governance of an aural/emotional/holistic response and the constraints of the literal content.

The lesson has reached a point where the blackboard is no longer a useful tool. A third column may be started, but fresh questions and closer scrutiny of parts will draw the class towards a more free-wheeling discussion format. Some of the puzzling aspects noted above may be directed to the students to work on in their discussion groups, to respond to in individual journal entries, or a combination of both (with the text available) with an optional whole-class take-up. In any event, the third column on the board may look something like this:

1. Tone / Mood   2. Content   3. Patterns
                                 (words, images, sounds)

    (as above)   spring / mud-luscious
                                          *
                                 balloonman / little lame
                                          *
                                 children / boys
                                 games / marbles / piracies
                                          *
                                 spring / puddle-wonderful
                                          *
                                 balloonman / queer old
                                          *
                                 children / girls
                                 games / hopscotch, jump-rope
                                          *
                                        etc.

Phase four: If and when the larger questions of who the balloonman is and what he is doing with or to the children are responded to by students, near the end of the phase-three discussion or following any group-work and/or journal response, a further activity remains an option: the poem could be read chorally to emphasize the gradations in tone, as confirmed by second reading. A recording of the poem read by the poet could be played and discussed: "Did he read it the way we've imagined it?" The visual effects of the poem on the page could be talked about in terms of fresh or confirmed meanings: "Did you expect 'eddieandbill' to be one word? Not capitalized? Does the capitalization of 'Man' alter your views of the balloonman and what he's doing?" And so on. If words like "innocence" and "evil" pop up (as they often do), then the wider allegorical implications of this theme — loss of innocence — might be broached. Again, do not push for this or force-feed it. More immediate and yet widening ripples of meaning should prove of interest, without the risk of suggesting to impressionable readers that poems are always tracked to thematic or allegorical dead ends. For example, ask here more natural questions like, "Is there any hint the children are moving willingly towards this Pan figure or are they ignoring him?" Reread the final lines and the syncopated and fading "far / and / wee," and let the students decide. Any study of the poem is complete only when a class feels it has explored it productively. They must get used to the notion that closure is always arbitrary, and the best way to achieve this is to say, "Well, we could go on, but why not take a few minutes now to write a summary comment in your response-journals" (with one or two prompts, perhaps, based on the questions still unanswered).

Resources

Poems are seldom "taught" in any conventional way before grades six or seven, as immersion and aesthetic extension are the principal teaching strategies, with occasional use, for advanced readers, of the informal reading methods outlined above. Much of the day-to-day pedagogy in the elementary school will naturally involve ways of using poetry to prompt students to write and perform their own or, in the primary grades, to assist with the teaching of reading itself. Hence, many of the resources for poetic writing listed in chapter 4 will be pertinent here as well. Also, while many of the teaching strategies that suit myths, legends and fairy tales are similar to those for poetry (especially in the early grades), resources for these have been placed in the chapter on fiction (pp. 96–100).

Linda Gibson Geller, *Word Play and Language Learning* (Urbana, IL: NCTE, 1985). A discussion with dozens of examples of how poems, riddles and nonsense verse help students from kindergarten to grade six learn to play with language, which in turn materially assists the development of literacy in general. An aesthetically rich pedagogy with specific, practical advice for teachers.

Carol Gillanders, *Theme and Image*, 2 vols. (Toronto: Copp Clark, 1968). The pair of teachers' guides that accompanied the original anthologies for the senior grades, while representative of the sixties' pedagogy that stressed second-reading analysis over first-reading response, are still repositories of interesting notes and useful questions and extension activities on dozens of classic poems often taught today. The analysis needs to be enriched by first-reading response and arranged to include group discussion in addition to any teacher-led lessons.

Don Gutteridge, *Brave Season: Reading and the Language Arts in Grades Seven to Ten* (London, ON: The Althouse Press, 1983). A sample lesson on a lyric poem is given on pages 187–189.

———, "The Ballads of Robin Hood: Listening To and Interpreting Poetry," in *English II: Speaking and Listening*, the Ontario Assessment Instrument Pool (Toronto: Ontario Ministry of Education 1981), 37–42. This is a fully detailed unit for grades seven to nine, with the focus on listening to a recording of the ballads and various response activities. A similar approach and unit of work appears in *English II* for act one of Shakespeare's *The Merchant of Venice*, for grade nine or ten (pp. 43 ff.).

———, "Shakespeare by Ear: *Macbeth* Through Listening and Discussion," *The English Exchange*, XVI, 1 (Autumn 1973) 11–16 and 33–37. The poetic-aesthetic qualities of Shakespeare's blank verse, the voices of the characters, and the dramatic nuances of their dialogue are highlighted in this listening-based methodology: a non-analytical way of introducing students to Shakespeare's dramatic poetry followed by a set of second-reading questions and a third-reading overview of themes.

Michael Hayhoe and Stephen Parker, *Words Large as Apples: Teaching Poetry 11–18* (Cambridge: Cambridge University Press, 1988). An eclectic collection of teaching methods and ideas, only some of which are aesthetic. The underlying theory is vaguely response- and student-centred.

Don Holdaway, *Stability and Change in Literacy Learning* (London, ON: The Althouse Press, 1983). Chapter 4 contains two complete units, one for emergent readers (kindergarten to grade one) and one for early readers (grade one to two), illustrating how to use poems and cloze exercises to teach phonics contextually, and how to set up and sequence lessons for a literacy-immersion kind of experience.

Robert Probst, *Response and Analysis: Teaching Literature in Junior and Senior High School* (Portsmouth, NH: Boynton/Cook/Heinemann, 1988). The chapters on poetry and the model lesson for grade nine (pp. 27–35) provide a balanced approach to response and analysis — that is, between first and second reading. The section on the novel and young adult literature, however, is both pedagogically and aesthetically weak. (See chapter 3 for a discussion of the particular challenge of teaching the novel while maintaining its aesthetic integrity.)

3

Aesthetic Reading: Fiction

Fiction and Why We Read It

Because short stories and novels are primarily aesthetic texts harbouring aesthetic intention, they share many of the qualities and aspects of poems. A discussion of what fiction is and how we ought to read it requires a brief recapitulation of the salient features of poetry and a detailed account of the few but significant differences between the two genres. Like poetry, fiction is composed by individuals, and invites the participation of a reader who comes to it with aesthetic expectation. The story it tells serves as the basic aesthetic motive, and is, like the feeling-thought of a poem, a unique configuration sprung from the imagination of a writer and presented to readers as a crafted text. As they do with poems, experienced readers take up a story-text freely and approach it aesthetically. While stories *can* be read efferently and analysed in various ways, most serious authors write for aesthetic readers.

Stories (I'll use this term to stand for the short story *and* the novel wherever convenient in this section) are fictional in the same sense that poems are: the story-thought or feeling-thought they present, latent in the text, does not purport to convey events, personages or emotions as they actually happened, as the news story of an earthquake might, replete with poetic-prose descriptions. Of course, they *might* have happened, but that is neither here nor there. The sophisticated reader expects a text that, when read aesthetically, will yield a virtual story, a uniquely shaped account of events, people and emotions that may or may not have actually occurred. Both writer and reader accept, in advance, that a fictional story is a species of make-believe. Any other assumption on the part of the reader will result in an efferent reading.

The aesthetic reader of stories, then, will also have to come to the text with a willing suspension of disbelief. If what is read has been invented or, in the least, reconfigured to reflect the writer's interest

Aesthetic Reading: Fiction 71

and bias, then an aesthetic reader will need to delay any skeptical interrogation of the unfolding events in the text until some sense of the whole story has been grasped. For stories are also whole structures and whole experiences, and always greater than the mere sum of their parts. As make-believe they may present us with elements of fantasy, dream life, and the surreal; they may play fast and loose with time and historical circumstance; and, while they are evolving towards closure, they may ask us to accept, however temporarily, values or implications about character and human behaviour that in other situations we would dismiss out of hand. Once the virtual story-as-a-whole has been grasped, suspension of disbelief is discontinued, as the story works its way into our consciousness, sensibility, and conscience — and thence into the world. All of the caveats and cautions suggested in chapter 2 about poetry and the poetry reader will apply equally to the story and its readers.

Stories also have ambiguity, but it is more likely to reside in the varying interpretations among readers than in the story or its intention. The kinds of short stories and novels that students are faced with in grades eleven and twelve are the exception to this rule, of course: the image-laden, symbolic and deftly narrated stories of a James Joyce or Alice Munro will present student-readers with deliberate and tantalizing ambiguities, which will require the same tactful handling by the teacher as the most complex poetry on the course. But the simpler, more narrative, more allegorical fiction preferred by younger students and their teachers (*The Light in the Forest, Moonfleet, Fahrenheit 451, Shane*) will give rise to open-ended discussions of motive and moral, and quiet reflection upon character and consequence in a response-journal. That is, most of the ambiguity will occur as the natural outcome of students' individual reactions to, and judgements of, the events of a story. The teacher, as we shall see, need only encourage the diversity while ensuring that students' responses have in fact been prompted by those events, by the virtual story itself. As with poetry, students should not be left with the notion that there is only one correct interpretation, so long as they have given the text their passionate attention and let it work aesthetically until its work is done.

The story as aesthetic text, however, differs in a number of respects from the poem, and raises several questions in its own right. Poetry presents itself to us as wrought language, and so, as we noted in chapter 2, we do not try to read through the words, syntax, and phrase/line structure (thus keeping them subsidiary while we work on what is being "said" to us), for a poem's language and structure are an inextricable part of its embodied meaning. Fiction, meanwhile, has as its basic aesthetic element not the word, as it were, but the story. It is not that its language — diction, tone, prose rhythms, dialogue — will not demand our attention from moment to moment, so much as it is that the virtual story we are building up or re-enacting in our heads as we go constitutes the primary aesthetic datum. Indeed, 'the story' is such a mesmerizing attraction for many young readers that they often *do* read through the surface language as if it were invisible, while focussing on the story they are deriving from it. Hence, they often require the assistance of a teacher to nudge them towards the story's rhetoric, particularly its descriptiveness and tone. Keep in mind, in this regard, that poems too have an evolving structure, signalled by rhetorical cues, but even though children come to primary school with a tacit verse-grammar and some of its rhetoric, these are varied and unpredictable. For instance, when we read a poem, the evolving structure (embedded narrative or drama, contrast, stanza "paragraphing," a statement made and rounded off) is part of our focal attention, but the possibilities for closure are limitless, and quite often we don't sense we are there until we have arrived.[1]

Story-grammar, however, is much more predictable, more deeply rooted, and more readily prompted to consciousness or tacit awareness. As we have seen, the verse rhythm is the hallmark of poetry, and is internalized as we learn to talk. The prose rhythm is the fundamental form of expression for the story and its base unit is the sentence.[2] But the acquisition and tacit storage of the sentences of the prose rhythm are not as direct or as unproblematic as the metrical line of the verse rhythm. The kind of sentence that two-year-olds learn is a prior and more flexible variant: the simple phrase of everyday speech, what Frye calls the associative rhythm and James Britton valorized in the term "expressive." As the basic unit of the associative rhythm, the speech-phrase is eminently suited to the many kinds of dialogue and casual talk that mark the social intercourse of humans from infancy on. For example, much of our daily conversation, even when we think we are being most coherent and pointed, is riddled with *ums* and *aahs*, backtracking, unfinished predicates, or worse. Nonetheless, our interlocutor is usually kind enough not to stop us and demand that we tidy up our syntax and utter only complete sentences and paragraphs.[3] (We will discuss the associative rhythm in more detail in chapter 4 when we examine expressive writing.)

The talk of preschoolers is thus a quaint combination of the elastic and syntactically forgiving speech rhythm and the lively, proto-aesthetic metrics of the verse rhythm; the latter achieves prominence during role play and schoolyard games and the former during more relaxed interchanges over lunch or in a discussion group arranged by the teacher. The true prose rhythm, whose basic unit is the grammatically ordered sentence, is not learned as an integral part of children's early speech acquisition but, rather, from exposure to stories read aloud to them by parents and others. When such exposure is repeated, intense and varied,[4] then the child will in fact internalize the sophisticated sentences of aesthetically-crafted stories at the same time as the language itself is being acquired under the impetus of the associative and verse rhythms. But thousands of children are read to very little or not at all; nor do they have psychologically and rhetorically powerful stories recited to them. (Fortunately almost every child achieves basic competence in the mother tongue.) The significance of all this for our understanding of the story-text and story reading is that internalization and storage in tacit form of aesthetic story-grammar will depend more on the preschooler's exposure to specific examples than will the acquisition of verse-grammar gained more generally. Similar exposure to nursery rhymes and poems for children will certainly enhance the latter, but even without it, there are still schoolyard games, skipping songs, chanted taunts and other environmental stimuli to reinforce the verse rhythm. In sum, the acquisition of sophisticated story-grammar is less certain and more contingent than verse-grammar.

This brings us to the question of narrative and story. Much has been written in the past fifty years on the subject, often with more zeal than clarity. For our purpose here, however, we will focus on how the differences between the two terms affect our conceptualization of the aesthetic and its unique features. The word "narrative" refers to the chronological arrangement of events with, more or less, some kind of beginning, middle and end. Quite properly, narrative[5] has been singled out by psychologists and epistemologists as an archetypal form of cognitive thought and its expression, as a way that human beings everywhere have of organizing the phenomena of the world. Some post-modernists view narrativity *per se* as an instrument of false order and control, but even such negative attention points to the fact of story's stubborn persistence in our lives. Phenomenology, for example, has deified the first-person narrative as the *only* valid method we have of building up concepts and generalizations.

Which is to say that narratives occupy a large space in our day-to-day conversations, and in our thoughts and dreams as well. The sketchiest account of what happened at recess or what you got for Christmas will take on the "and ... and ... and" pattern of arrangement and will, most of the time, have some sort of beginning (however abrupt) and, should we not be rudely interrupted, some rounding off or closure (however feeble). So deeply and tacitly understood is this basic format that children will often utter such narratives in tandem, alternating events with ease. It is fair to conclude, then, that even when formal stories are *not* read to them from books, children acquire a profound knowledge of rudimentary narrative and its social function. Most often, though, these narratives of our everyday conversation are dominated more by the halting or breathless associative rhythm than by the syntactic and rhetorical niceties of the prose sentence.

But is a simple recounting to friends of some adventure we experienced on our holidays not a story? Not in the narrow, aesthetic context we have been exploring. In order for it to achieve the status of aesthetic text or art-speech, two conditions must first be met. It must convey a sense that it has been crafted and shaped, so that if it were to be repeated later on ("Say, Jack, tell us that wonderful story of you and the grizzly again!") it would be retold in much the same manner — tone, sequence of events, dramatic pauses, mimicked voices — and with most of the same words and sentences. Secondly, the crafting and shaping should prompt aesthetic pleasure in the listener; for example, the story pleasures of anticipation, confirmation or surprise, tension and relief, empathy with character and viewpoint, conflict and resolution, and the "rightness" of the language carrying the flow of the story to us. Surely this is what we have in mind when we say that so-and-so is a born storyteller, a person who can take a prolix and limp anecdote of conversational discourse and retell it as if it were a family legend or a spoken text on the precipice of print. So it is that we readily forgive the master storyteller any story-enhancing hyperbole or dramatic conflation of events or tidy departures from what actually occurred. At this point we are on the verge of attributing to such a crafted account the final criterion of the fully aesthetic text: it is *made up*, an acceptable reconfiguration of what happened to induce aesthetic pleasure and urge upon us a kind of meaning unique to that story. Here, also, we are invited to honour the truth of artifice over reality.

Just as poems embody for us one-of-a-kind presentations of feeling-thought, so too do short stories and novels offer us a specialized and untranslatable form of knowledge, and that knowledge is situated chiefly in the story elements (as above), which include the language used to bring them to the reader but to a lesser extent than for poems. Language is primary in poetry and patterning or structure secondary. The profound tacit knowledge that some children have of basic story-grammar — and *all* children have of rudimentary narrative — permits them, as soon as they learn to decode print efficiently, to begin devouring storybooks and simple novels on their own. Furthermore, the more sophisticated stories read aloud to them by their teachers increase the complexity and range of tacit rhetorical understandings. In reading aesthetic texts and having them read to us, we *always* know more than we can say, and are internalizing, for future use, information we are not consciously aware of.

Yet, how *can* the unique meaning of a crafted story-text lie in its story elements? Surely any meaning we take from a story is rooted in our response to, and opinion of, its characters, what they say and do, and whatever values they espouse or enact. In other words, it is the content that we turn to when someone asks us, "What do you think Alice Munro is telling us about love in 'How I Met My Husband'?" But, of course, there is no true content outside the story itself. The events, and the characters in them, have been arranged for us with only those aspects of either element the writer wishes to include. The result is that what is told and what is left out that might have been told, are equally critical to our understanding of what is happening, of the "point" that the narrative parts (included and omitted) are "making" when we let them add up to something more than the cumulative total. Moreover, the narrative point of view in most sophisticated story-texts is itself restricted and the narrator may be a key player in the events as they unfold, or may be unreliable, biased or deliberately ambivalent. Much of this will be conveyed to us by tone or "voice," by the timbre and rhythm of word and sentence, by subtle rhetorical cues, or by embedded imagery and symbol. In brief, from the straightforward adventure novel aimed at grade-fours to the elegant intricacies of Munro or Katherine Mansfield, what we take away from a story, beyond the aesthetic pleasures of a first reading, is an account of something that happened (fictionally) for which we have some personal referents and associations. It is, however, an account that, even when it is about events or behaviours with which we are very familiar, has been arranged and deliberately narrated in non-synonymous language. It is this *arrangement* and its special effect on our emotions, sympathies and moral sensibility that produces the kind of experience only obtained from stories.

Put another way, short stories and novels, like poems, are not vicarious experiences so much as they are a unique and irreplaceable *form* of experience. In re-enacting them as readers we live through event, characterization and plot in the present tense, even as the narrative flows by into the virtual past. The essential aesthetic meaning, then, lies in our participation in a story about something derived from our natural propensity to narrate the world, but reordered and shaped and made metaphoric because it is shot through with "what if" and "suppose" and "once upon a time." In working up a story-text into something more than a word chronicle, in re-enacting the virtual story that exists only as a product of the particular arrangement — of character, event, narration, description — we enter into, however fleetingly, a way of seeing and feeling we can achieve by no other means. Is this not what we mean when we say that we get "lost" in a novel? And because aesthetic stories have the familiar ring of everyday anecdote and deal with recognizable people, places and happenings, they seem merely to heighten, sharpen and intensify what we already half know. They have the capacity to ease into our consciousness and settle there, the myths and values embedded in them subtly transforming us. In this sense, short stories and novels — often bearing the patina of everyday life — can be more subversive than poetry, whose aesthetic features are foregrounded and forewarning. They can also immeasurably expand our awareness of the world and one another.[6]

As with poems, readers may choose to pull out bits of stories — character A's pithy aphorisms, the way character B handled herself in a certain situation, a well-wrought phrase, a descriptive passage, a riposte to character C's provocative assertion, the author's unintended chauvinism — and use them as we wish, but in doing so at the expense of reading the virtual story and reflecting upon it, we have made a decision to read the text efferently. Many novels and short stories reward both efferent and aesthetic readings; it is only when efferent reading (where the text is treated as if it were discursive) is mistaken for or confused with aesthetic reading that the latter becomes impossible. We also need to remember that any rhetorically rich and well-arranged story has most assuredly been composed to appeal to and reward an aesthetic response.

We have, then, a definition of what constitutes an aesthetic story-text, an explanation of the kind of knowledge it will yield when approached sympathetically, and a description of the qualities and expectations of a "right reader." We are now ready to look at the actual cognitive process the reader will use.[7]

The Process of Reading Fiction

The process by which all aesthetic story-text is comprehended differs from the poetry-reading process in one significant way. Because the aesthetic aspect of a poem resides in the very presence and tone of its language, the reader must hear it — read aloud, subvocalized, heard in the mind — a procedure that slows the otherwise peripheral processing of the letters and words in order that the full impact and meaning of the evolving feeling-thought can remain focal. In reading a story, the decoding of letter and word and basic syntax (the surface text) remains peripheral, along with any long-familiar story cues that hover at the edge of tacit awarenesss; for example, "It all began when ...," "Charlotte would often *leave* her web ... but *today* she *was* too busy ...," "Fern *recalled when* she ...," "*Meanwhile, back in* the barn ...." As a result, the reader is free to focus on two conscious concerns: following the narrative flow as it unfolds (what is happening now?) and using it to anticipate and build up an emergent virtual story (What is *really* going on here? ... Where *is* this thing going? ... Oh, I didn't expect *that!* ... My, the heroine seems likeable, I hope she ...) Much of the aesthetic pleasure on first reading centres on the tension between "what is happening?" and "what is really happening?" with all its concomitant delights: empathy, suspense, anxiety and relief, anticipation and confirmation or surprise, symmetry of event, rightness of language, and resolution and closure.

In the kind of straight-ahead novels many primary and middle-school students select for independent reading, the surface is read peripherally and the narrative line and flow kept in focus, as rudimentary narrative-aesthetic pleasures are savoured while driving the emergent story forward. With early narrative readers, there will be little difference between the unfolding narrative and the virtual story, partly because the novels they choose are often written for them and feature first-person narration (usually a youthful protagonist), chronological sequencing and plot-based conflict. Any story-rhetoric — subtle cues regarding the reliability of the narrator, meaningful descriptive language, shifts in tense or voice — is underemphasized so as not to distract. If these cues were overly obtrusive or integral to the narrative flow, the inexperienced reader might abandon the book.

Blips and brief productive pauses cause the focal-peripheral positions to be reversed, in milliseconds, but do not normally impede either comprehension or aesthetic pleasure. As soon as some word or phrase in the printed text disturbs the narrative flow — it could be an unfamiliar word or a referent not immediately recognized — the reader focusses on this surface text while the narrative flow recedes momentarily to the periphery of consciousness. If the zone of tacit awareness contains a solution to the question raised or suggests, from the context, that any resolution can be safely held in abeyance, then a mere blip is felt, as the emerging story becomes the focal concern again. Any explicit search of the store of tacit knowledge (life knowledge or rhetoric knowledge) or casting back to earlier events in the story, however, will result in a noticeable pause, interrupting the flow more significantly. If the search is successful, the reader happily returns to the focal concern: the pause has been productive. If the search has been unsuccessful or too prolonged, the pause may impede the comprehension process, momentarily or permanently.

Even, however, when this normal comprehension process is moving along, smoothly or bumpily, readers — including inexperienced basic narrative readers — are seldom kept at the painstaking business of active reading solely by the simple narrative pleasures of suspense, anticipation, etc. In the romance novel, the format young readers prefer,[8] a major element of the story will be a hero with whom the youngster (usually of the same gender) identifies, and who often tells his or her own story, and with whose values and fate the reader becomes bound up. Even at the most elementary level, a novel is always more than the recitation of its narrative parts.

The chief difference between basic-narrative readers and more advanced, enriched readers of story-text is that the latter have probably chosen a story where the pure pleasures of narrative movement are enhanced by meaningful and suggestive description, subtle shifts in tone or angle of narration, and abbreviated dialogue calling for more inference. Within the evolving narrative flow and emergent virtual story, the advanced reader will experience millisecond shifts of focal-peripheral awareness between the narrative flow and the rhetoric, all the while reading through the surface print. Productive pauses and blips will be occasioned at the surface, in the story-rhetoric, or in the narrative flow itself. Further discussion of these enriched-story readers appears below.

It seems either miraculous or incredible that such an intricate process should be manipulated by almost all the students who learn to decode print in emergent and early reading programmes. And the hypotheses put forward here are merely a crude guess at the sort of things that must happen if we are to explain how young untutored readers achieve what they so obviously do. For example, moves like the near-instantaneous loopbacks to earlier events or words, and the leaping ahead where readers predict what may happen, go on continuously and naturally — peripherally wherever possible — while the focal-subsidiary processing of immediate text is proceeding apace. Nor could the most gifted teacher conceive of explicitly instructing grade threes in how to go about such focal-peripheral switching and productive pausing and in the making explicit of tacit knowledge as needed and its suppression when not. We know that even in assisting beginners to decipher print, too much direct instruction or the premature imposition of phonics rules or morphological cues may jeopardize the enterprise itself.[9] Believable or not, by grade four most students are able to sit still long enough to be absorbed in an exciting novel close to their interests and experience — imaginative experience, I hasten to add. None of which is to imply that there is no role for teaching. Quite the contrary, as we shall see below. But our teaching must take into account that the elementary process of comprehension of story-text has generally been acquired by grade four, and that, where it hasn't, the decoding of the surface (the line of print) has probably remained overly focal, and thus debilitating to any focussed evocation of the narrative flow.

Before we move on to the pedagogical principles to be extrapolated from this theory of fiction reading, it may be useful to mention briefly a few more of the advanced moves characteristic of the maturing reader, particularly because they may point to teaching strategies for middle-school and senior students.

Story-Line Reflection: During natural breaks in the story line (chapter, section, "scene"), the reader consciously reflects back on the story so far, deepening the aesthetic pleasures of empathy (with main characters, situation, value positions), prediction (what might happen), and living through other experience (reviewing and savouring again favourite sections). Reflective pauses may add to the questions already raised and these may hover in the zone of tacit awareness until the next pause. An implicit sense of narrative chunking is essential if reflective pauses are to be productive rather than distractive.

Associative Reflection: Because the emergent story-in-the-head is built up virtually from the active processing of the words and experiential referents of the text out of the store of life knowledge (some of it tacit) and rhetoric knowledge (most of it tacit), the reader — in imagining the events — may be struck by associative connections well beyond the focal pursuit of story. For example, a family crisis in the novel may reflect a recent one in the reader's own home and a reverie of pleasurable or painful memories be initiated. For the advancing basic-narrative reader, this kind of association is essential to growth in the normal fiction-reading process and, in the form of a reflective pause (as above), it can serve to deepen the aesthetic pleasure of empathy as the pursuit of story is resumed. If overly prolonged or too freely associative, however, it can make re-entry into the narrative flow more difficult by providing too focal a concern too soon. Fully mature readers, who can hold more of the emergent virtual story in their head, are able to free-associate more indulgently with more likelihood of applying any such personal meanderings to the evolving story.

Skimming / Editing: In pursuit of the virtual story, the reader may choose, whenever a pause occurs, not to shift the focus to a search for answers to the question raised, but rather decide to skim through or skip over the puzzling section (often descriptive chunks for inexperienced readers). The story-so-far is held peripheral and tacit while the focal task is switched to discovering the extent of the interruption (e.g., a full paragraph of thick description) until the narrative line clearly re-enters the text (likely in the form of a clear stretch of action or dialogue), and normal reading resumes. If the reader becomes lost, he or she may, of course, pause and go back over the skimmed chunk to determine if some thread has been inadvertently skipped over. Some readers will be so skilled at such editing, especially with highly predictable texts, that there will be little or no interference with anticipated aesthetic pleasure. The difference between mature and inexperienced readers in this regard is that mature readers are capable of skimming seemingly interruptive chunks to grasp their general effect and make certain that there are no details essential to the main narrative. They will also eventually come to realize the importance, in sophisticated fiction, of descriptive and atmospheric passages. That is, they will know when to skim and when not to.

Advance Preparation: Maturing readers may think about the novel they have selected before beginning to read. They may be able to anticipate a great deal about the story-to-come from the blurb, the cover illustration, title, author, or genre-category, enhanced by previous reading of a similar nature or by information supplied by the teacher, other students or the librarian. Whether such intimations are explicit or tacit, they will provide a predictive framework that will expand the zone of tacit awareness during reading and intensify aesthetic pleasure, but only if the advanced frame of prediction does not become overly focal to the point where it distorts the more natural pursuit of story.[10]

Tolerance / Holding-in-Abeyance: When the reader is compelled to make a pause — to get a story or rhetoric question resolved by shifting the focus of attention to readily accessible stores of tacit knowledge — more often than not, no immediate or completely satisfying answer will present itself, nor will attempts to self-prompt the needed information or understanding from deeper sources be successful. This is especially true early in the first reading of stories and novels, when so little is known and so much promised. At such times the reader may wish to resort to a reflective scan of earlier aspects of the story (a sophisticated move) or merely decide that the pursuit of story is still worthwhile, that it has not been irremediably harmed by the unresolved question which may, indeed, be an intrinsic part of the story's unfolding. Suspense and mystery, for example, operate on this shared assumption between fiction writer and aesthetic reader. So the unresolved question is held in abeyance, not to be forgotten but kept peripheral in the zone of tacit awareness, where it is ready to be used later on. Such a tolerance for unresolved questions at appropriate points is an essential aspect of growth in the aesthetic reading of fiction. I suspect that it is nurtured by past successful experiences with whole-story interpretation. For mature readers the search for an answer is often brief and the abeyance manoeuvre initiated even before any extensive pause or reflection is tried. That is, the unconscious prediction provided so naturally here allows many apparently critical story/rhetoric questions to be incorporated *unanswered* into the focal pursuit of story. In truth, they become part of the pursuit itself, and add immensely to aesthetic satisfaction. We allow ourselves to be tantalized, mystified, intrigued, or made skeptical: by the storyline and, for advanced readers, by rhetorical patterns evolving parallel to, in concert with, and as potential meaning for, the ongoing story.

These advanced moves are, of course, refinements on the basic focal-peripheral process, not a discrete set of skills to be directly taught or learned in specialized academic courses in the senior grades. However, together with an understanding of the primary cognitive mechanism, they do allow us to hypothesize how progress, or growth, in fiction reading occurs. (A not dissimilar one would operate for poetry reading.)

Growth in aesthetic reading is not merely a result of learning more generic and rhetorical information or more devices, terms and moves. The basic process does not change, or ought not to. The pursuit of story remains the primary aesthetic purpose and pleasure, and the focal-peripheral processing — with, most likely, the addition of more productive pauses and reflections — remains unchanged also. What *has* changed in the maturing reader, as a result of gains in life knowledge and in interpretive reading experiences of an appropriate kind, is the range of accessible meanings in the virtual story. The conception of what constitutes plot, more subtle means of characterization, value- and theme-laden event, embedded symbolism, and much more has been "thickened" by years of reading experience and by conceptual extrapolations made therefrom. Thus the more advanced reader approaches, say, a classic novel with more elaborate expectations of what the virtual story is likely to yield.

Moreover, the amount of readily available rhetorical information in the tacit store is greater, and is more conceptually refined and ready for use with even larger, more tacit, internalized stores in reserve. Nonetheless, though some or much of this rhetoric knowledge may now be explicitly known, it is still kept wherever possible at the periphery of the reading process in the zone of tacit awareness, where it acts to facilitate and materially enrich normal aesthetic reading, and remains there to become focal only when required. The processing mechanism *per se* has not changed. Put another way, the advanced processing of a particular reader can only be assessed in terms of the *actual moves while reading (rereading / reflecting on) a specific, text*, and, conversely, can never be assessed purely by the amount of explicit rhetorical and generic knowledge displayed out of the context of normal aesthetic reading. In brief, knowing about devices and moves is not the same as using them. Hence, if rhetoric knowledge becomes overly focal or disembodied from the pursuit of story, or dominates reflective moments, or is deployed self-consciously as an "advance frame," then the reader may be doing *some* kind of reading, but it won't be aesthetic.

Pedagogical Principles and Implications for Teaching Fiction

Much of the groundwork for thinking about how we can best approach the teaching of fiction has already been laid in the discussion of poetry in chapter 2. What follows is a consideration of the six pedagogical principles enumerated there as they might apply to the teaching of short stories and novels, with emphasis upon any marked differences between the two.

The first principle suggested that teachers must themselves be readers, and must fully understand the aesthetic nature of poems and the particular process of reading they excite. The same principle will apply in the case of stories. And because the aesthetic-reading process for stories is not exactly the same as for poems, though sharing many features unique to aesthetic reading, those differences must be acknowledged and used to guide our teaching. Of critical importance is the fact that the basic aesthetic satisfaction in reading fiction is derived from the configuration of story elements as virtual story and, unlike poetry, only secondarily from the language, however poetic. One simple way of demonstrating the primacy of story is to reflect upon the motives and pleasures associated with students' obsessive interest in TV shows and movies, the vast majority of which are narrative-based. (The more recent interest of adolescents in the short, semi-surreal music video suggests also that the lyric poem is not moribund.) Students obviously achieve aesthetic satisfaction from the plots of sitcoms and action-flicks alike — where the conventional elements of narrative and rudimentary story are almost always present — and from bonding with familiar character-types who treat viewers to suspense, anticipation, surprise or confirmation, tension and relief, and so on. These are the staples of the story-form in its innumerable manifestations in our culture,[11] which explains why our students' knowledge of non-linguistic story-elements, both conscious and tacit, is wide-ranging and deeply internalized. Basic story-grammar in its infinite variations is played out before them a dozen times every day. Even without an extensive reading base, then, most students will intuitively comprehend a rudimentary story and respond to its aesthetic constituents, its pleasures, and its potential insight into human behaviour.

This phenomenon must be taken into account by teachers at all levels, but is especially important in the upper-middle and senior grades. There, for example, it is easy for teachers of advanced readers to forget that the meaning and the pleasure in reading short stories and novels is rooted in their story values. As these texts become more rhetorically complex and less blatantly narrative in their structure and movement, teachers may be tempted to overemphasize the niceties of descriptive-symbolic imagery, ambiguity in angle of narration, disjunctive chronology, and thematic evocation (among other devices) at the expense of conventional story elements. After all, advanced readers will have both the vocabulary and prior reading experience to permit them entry into the rarefied air of classic adult fiction. Increasing exposure to more challenging texts, however, though a legitimate goal for senior English classes, must be orchestrated in such a way as to be seen by students as an extension and enrichment of the fundamental story-values they have come to enjoy — not a new, academic game.

Conversely, when dealing with younger readers in grades six to nine or with basic-narrative readers in grades ten to twelve, teachers are apt to overlook the students' reservoir of internalized story knowledge (non-linguistic), and consequently belabour the study of a short story or novel with redundant tasks like plot graphing, chapter précis, and superficial queries about what happened. Such tautologies are inevitably distracting to students (who often resist them and hence convince their teachers that they need more of this kind of work, not less). They also suggest to students that first reading is not a natural response to story-level inferences and accompanying pleasures, but rather a halting, fragmented over-focussing upon bits and pieces of bewildering information. If these students cannot infer the basic storyline and enjoy the piece at some level of satisfaction during an engaging read-aloud, then the material itself is patently too difficult, in its rhetoric or its life-experience, and has been inappropriately chosen. By the same token, if a grade-twelve gifted group cannot read a classic novel like Faulkner's The Sound and the Fury, after a suitable introductory engagement, without disruptive and over-focussed attention to literal story elements, then it is counter-productive to plod through any detailed analysis on second reading in the faint hope that an analytical effort will make the story comprehensible and appreciated. *Aesthetic and emotional engagement must be* achieved in some reasonable way before any analysis of parts is begun.

The second principle will be of assistance here: the teacher must arrange for and ensure a fully aesthetic first reading. Just because students may be capable of taking home a whole-class core novel and reading it on a weekend, does not imply that we should let them do so — without some guarantee that they will be engaging it aesthetically. Psychologically powerful and rhetorically intricate novels, the kind often chosen for whole-class study, will normally require the teacher to present them initially in a context that honours the language, the rhetoric, and the story-elements. Hence, most anthologized short fiction should be read aloud or presented on recording so that the linguistic-rhetorical features are heard; the first few chapters of a core novel should be similarly introduced, even in the most advanced senior classes. Having students respond immediately, via point-form jottings or brief journal entries, to the cued or uncued read-aloud will signal to students that first-reading pleasures and initial responses are not merely valid *per se*, but are helpful in setting up subsequent readings. The novel is particularly challenging in this regard because there is the risk during a read-aloud of the early chapters that second-reading questions will arise to slow any initial, unconstrained responses and, alas, distort and devalue them. At some judicious point, students will need to be sent home, novel in hand, with instructions to finish it. Ideally, the teacher's introduction will have piqued their interest and provided just enough intimation about tone, point of view, and emerging conflict to propel them through the remainder of the novel. Even so, the use of calculated journal prompts at key points in the novel will allow first-reading responses to be recorded and used later to frame any second-reading analysis. (The sample lesson and the resource section below provide examples of these methods.)

The chief difference between the teaching of fiction to advanced students (enriched-story readers) and those less advanced (basic-narrative readers) will be in the selection of core texts for whole-class study and the teacher's decision, as in poetry lessons, as to how far to pursue second reading (if at all), as well as the rhetorical focus of any such questions. With basic-narrative readers and a selection of less demanding novels and stories, the most effective pedagogy is likely to be an engaging introduction, some independent reading in class and at home, with journal prompts to elicit initial responses and impressions, and a reflective reading in which those responses form the basis for whole-class and group discussion of the story, its characters, and any issues it might raise. Many aesthetically based teaching materials are available and are listed in the resource section; what we are doing here is exploring the *general* implications for teaching to be drawn from the elaborated theory.

It is when we move from the business of appropriate selection to the fourth principle, i.e., if, when and how second reading is to be carried out, that close adherence to the implications of our theory is obligatory, regardless of grade or programme. In the primary school we do not have to worry about this because, once again, immersion and aesthetic extension are the watchwords with read-alouds by teacher and students, dramatizations, and free-wheeling follow-up talk dominating lessons. When students begin to read novels independently, however, teachers will need to encourage, in a variety of ways, as much individualized reading as possible — with some third-reading extension and follow-up, like book talks, journal entries, and group projects — while at the same time feeding the tacit stores of story knowledge by reading, with the whole class, novels and stories that are rhetorically and linguistically richer than those being read out of class. Any tentative introduction to second reading will not focus explicitly on these rhetorical-linguistic complexities (they need to be internalized and kept tacit long before any conscious study) but on a second look at the motives of characters, personal responses to any ambiguities in their behaviour and, tactfully, emerging themes. The latter, almost always in grades four to seven, are cast in the form of values conflict and resolution; for example, character A finally learns to temper her overweening pride.

Even so, second reading in the short story or novel, however tactful its introduction, is inherently more difficult to manage than it is for the lyric poem. A poem-text is a visible construct, viewable on a single page, an overhead transparency or the blackboard. Short stories unfold over half a dozen or more pages, and novels over hundreds, making their structure less visible. Moreover, the aesthetic features of poetry can be revisited visually in seconds, and relevant sections or the whole can be read aloud without students losing their place. Such a tidy re-examination of selected parts cannot be similarly managed for the short story or the novel, and the whole — the emergent virtual story — can be seen only in the mind and memory of the students. When the teacher begins to lead students back from their first responses, and the unresolved questions raised by them, to have a second look at pertinent parts of the story, it will be far too easy to become bogged down or lost in those parts, or to begin treating them as if they existed relatively independently of the whole. For example, if the motives of character A in situation B require a rereading to be resolved or understood, teachers can be forgiven if they focus relentlessly on that section of the text until some consensus of opinion is achieved. Far worse is the tendency to rush prematurely to a thematically revealing segment or statement near the end of the text in an effort to stimulate interest and incite class discussion.

What is really happening here, and in any other overfocussed scrutiny of parts, is that the fragments are likely being studied with only a token nod at the story-elements as a whole. We noted above that both aesthetic satisfaction and the unique meaning of fiction derive from its story structure. As with poetry, the content or bits of it cannot be pulled out and treated as if they held independent import, unless the reader wishes to switch the reading posture from aesthetic to efferent. And because a story is usually composed of a sequence of separate incidents, it is tempting to view them as if they were mini-stories in and of themselves. But the full, aesthetically unique meaning of short stories and novels inheres in the arrangement of incidents, in the characters embedded in and propelling them, and in the language and angle of narration used to funnel this arrangement to the reader. It is, as I have theorized, this particular configuration of events — and its depiction of actions, people, settings and situations putatively drawn here and there from the real world — that is the meaning of any story. If we need to examine character A's motives in situation B, we must do so in light of any *previously* pertinent detail and with a view to helping explain *subsequent* actions and eventual resolutions.

In practice, this requires teachers to carry out second-reading analyses, in general, by selecting and highlighting segments in the order of their appearance in the flow of the story, and with some explicit or implicit looping back and forward to contingent events. A random, hodgepodge selection of highlights may promote lots of bubbling talk in class and lead to the thematic and content-based pursuits of third-reading extension; but these will be premature, and devastating to aesthetic pleasure and its embodied truths. Many recent teacher guides on literature, for example, suggest that students actually learn to read novels and plays best when they stop after every chapter to carry out a bewildering array of self-selected extension activities.[12] This procedure, which effectively substitutes third reading for second, also guarantees that no legitimate first reading of the whole will occur; moreover, it treats second reading as an arbitrary exercise in doing other things with language than actually rereading the text. Proper second reading is in fact a further and more profound form of cognitive processing, with its own attendant pleasure and insight.

With advanced readers in grades ten to twelve, the challenge of second reading for fiction is much the same as it is for poetry: to gauge the right time and level of explicitness in introducing the more sophisticated aspects of story rhetoric and language. The governing principle is still the maintenance of aesthetic integrity, which in practice means keeping discussion of the formal rhetoric — or devices, to use the more common term — either implicit or clearly connected to the more experiential story values. I have written elsewhere and extensively on the formulation and sequencing of second- and third-reading questions on the novel, and refer the reader to items in the resource section below; in addition, the sample lesson on the piece by Farley Mowat is meant to illustrate the process near the midpoint of the middle years: grade six or seven.

When we come to third reading and the principle governing it, we find significant differences between poetry and fiction. As noted in chapter 2, third reading of a poem often occurs naturally as a rounding off of second reading, a putting-together-again, as it were, of the examined parts. Third-reading extensions of individual poems are usually personal summary responses or aesthetic transpositions: writing a poem, choral performance, private reflection in journals. It is only when poems are grouped in sustained units that full extensions into thematic or generic elaboration are made feasible, and desirable. But the novel invites third-reading activities in and of itself. The kinds of core novels we select for whole-class study are by definition both rhetorically rich and thematically reverberant. By the time an advanced grade ten or eleven class has reached, on second reading, the two-thirds point of, say, *To Kill a Mockingbird*, the themes of racial discrimination, coming of age, and gender prejudice have begun to emerge in increasing complexity, and start to raise thorny and ambivalent questions about values, human behaviour and social issues. Second reading, in a sense, has turned automatically into a form of third reading. That is the way the best stories work, configuring and sequencing events so that questions of value surface slowly and inexorably, and call for our considered and earnest response. They do not, however, float free of the story: the racial-prejudice theme of *Mockingbird* cannot be fully separated from Scout's narration of it (we have it almost exclusively from her viewpoint) or from the coming-of-age theme that she and Jem embody, for it is racial and gender prejudice and its manifold manifestations in her home town that compel her to move from the innocence of childhood to troubling maturity, which transformation includes recognition of her own prejudging of Boo Radley. We can pull out discrete strands for temporary and convenient scrutiny, but we need to put them back as well if students are to apprehend the true complexity of the novel, both its realism and its metaphoric possibility. Moreover, the tug on our sympathies, achieved by the language and point of view, is an important aspect of the mix, so much so that our initial responses on first reading may be tempered, altered or confirmed on subsequent readings. One way or another, such aesthetic devices will colour our final opinions on any questions raised. In sum, the third-reading end-discussion of a whole-class novel study is like no other in the school curriculum. It must not be approached as if it were a branch of social studies or a religion class or a project in Health.

Once the whole novel has been read aesthetically and so discussed, further third-reading activities are possible. They include comparative work, in discussion groups or as independent study, with other novels or stories by the same author, on the same theme(s), or of the same genre. Here, too, extensions ought to take advantage of the fully-realized readings of the original novel or unit of stories. Novels, however, often have minor themes, and these can be used to prompt extension activities in essay writing, additional reading, projects, dramatizations, and so on. When such parts of a novel are used, the activities often slip over into fourth reading; that is, the original stimulus is just that: it does not carry over to, or seriously constrain, the subsequent work. For example, after reading in class *The Piano Man's Daughter* by Timothy Findley, one student might choose to do a history of piano making in Canada or North America, prompted but not constrained by the section on piano manufacturing in the novel. Finally, as with poetry, such analyses should be initiated only with advanced senior classes and after the completion of three aesthetic readings, in order that aesthetic response and aesthetically presented meaning be allowed to operate untrammelled by any contradictory, second-order entanglement.

Before we turn to the sample lesson and list of resources, one last general notion should receive due attention. Many official curriculum guidelines justify the inclusion of imaginative literature, and the novel in particular, in English courses on the grounds that it provides youngsters with *vicarious experience*, and by logical extension gives them access to cultural and historical information in a pleasing and palatable format. While we have already noted the dangers of the content fallacy latent in the latter claim, the concept of vicarious experience is widely bruited and solemnly cherished by English teachers themselves. For good reason. Young people and adults alike tell us that they experience the illusion of entering another world when they attend a performance of *Lear* or *Hamlet*, or enthuse about getting blissfully lost in an engrossing novel. The popularity of historical fiction, historical romance, and historically-set mystery novels speaks to the same point, and adds to it the satisfaction of learning about other times and places while we are immersed in narrative delights. But the contribution of novel reading to cultural and historical learning is educationally justified only as long as these satisfactions remain integrated — as they are in the novels we select for core study — and as long as students realize that facts embedded in fictional narrative are presented to create a particular effect and fed to the reader through affecting prose and distorting narrative technique.

In this context, "vicarious" is a slightly misleading term, for it implies an experience "in place of." "In place of *what*?" we might well ask. In place of real-life experience seems the obvious answer; but it is not a valid one. Real-life experience cannot be replicated, nor can it ever be adequately represented in works of art, not even in the stories told on film with apparently real settings and mobile, talking human beings. What we see in artfully crafted movies and the best novels are events reconfigured by artifice into a virtual story that gives us the illusion that it represents actual events but which is, by mutual agreement between maker and responder, a concocted version of them; this offers readers everywhere the opportunity of assimilating a kind of experience and form of knowledge unique in the world. In the case of fiction, the assimilation is literal because readers must activate the aesthetic cues and re-enact the virtual story by making the suggested associations and referents from their own lives. In this way, literature is both virtual and actual, and is so much more than a weak stand-in for experiences we might one day be brave enough to encounter on our own. We learn from literature what we can never learn from life, and vice versa. I can think of no more compelling reason for making it the centrepiece of the humanities curriculum.

A Sample Lesson

The lesson outlined below might take two or more actual class periods, depending on which optional moves are selected by the teacher according to the needs of individual classes. The story, actually an excerpt from Farley Mowat's *The Curse of the Viking Grave*,¹³ has been chosen as part of a longer unit of stories on a theme like "Growing Up: Girls and Boys" and/or "Growing Up in Different Cultures." Because this incident is strongly narrative with its themes well embedded, it serves nicely as an engaging initial text for such a unit, and one especially appropriate to basic-narrative readers in grade six or seven. The lesson plan has been designed to allow for both the gender and culture versions of growing up to emerge. The particularly aesthetic features of the pedagogy to note are:

- the aesthetic presentation of the initial read-aloud, where the teacher and/or students (who might prepare sections in advance) present the story in a dramatic fashion; this can either be all the way through without interruption or with pauses only at the end of dramatic sequences or in scenes, interspersed with quick, story-enhancing questions;
- the open-ended, personal-response prompts for individual student writing in journals, during and after first reading;
- the use of a Canadian-authored text with a cultural theme of particular relevance to Canadian experience and a gender-based theme that should appeal to preadolescent youngsters;
- the careful balancing of textual meaning (the content and rhetoric of the story) and textual interpretation by the students in:
  (1) the second-reading questions (text-focussed / interpretively open-ended),
  (2) the open-ended third-reading questions,
  (3) the small-group discussion used to stimulate and validate the open-endedness,
  (4) the extension of the story through a personal, reflective journal response, and
  (5) the attention given *throughout* to the stage that the readers are in (age, reading experience, and linguistic ability) through the choice of text, the wording of the tasks, and the sequencing of teacher-led to student-led to individual summary activities.

EXPERIENTIAL INTRODUCTION
(Optional. Focus on students' prior experience)

1. How many of you have been on a canoe trip? Where did you go? What did you take along? What are some of the hazards? What skills are required? etc.

2. Where are the Barren Lands of Canada? Fort Churchill? What would the landscape up there be like? etc.

FIRST READING
(Focus on first impressions, personal response, experiential story values)

This is a teacher-led shared reading and first response to the story. The read-aloud may be interrupted briefly, where appropriate, for the teacher to ask basic-narrative questions of the "what happened or is about to happen?" variety. The interim journal activity may be used independently or combined with basic questioning. After the read-aloud, the teacher leads the class in a brief overview of the story, capturing the cumulative first responses and inciting speculation about potential areas of interest with the intention of drawing out students' impressions of characters, key events, and outcome (wherein the themes lie embedded). This should be open-ended, with no blackboard summary or redirection into the text. The end-of-story journal prompt may be used to assist the overview, especially if individual responses are desired; for example, where there is a surprise ending.

Overview Questions:
1. What made this an especially dangerous kind of canoe trip?
2. What parts of the story were most exciting for you?
3. What actions in the story, if any, surprised you? Seemed strange or almost impossible?
4. How old do you think the characters were? What gave you this impression?

Optional Journal Prompts:
1. Preparatory / Interim: After first reading of pp. 27 to 30, line 1 ("... to lift a paddle"):

- Do you think Jamie may be making a mistake taking Angeline along? Give your opinion. (3 minutes)

The teacher conducts a brief survey of volunteer responses, remembering not to explore reasons in depth. Discussion is kept speculative and personal. "Well, let's see ..." and the read-aloud is continued. Optionally, journal responses may be left until the read-aloud is completed, and used to focus the brief overview and/or lead students back into some aspect of second reading.

2. Response to the Whole Text: On completion of first reading of the story, students are given *one* of these prompts (determined by the unit-themes or needs of the students at a particular moment):
- Whom did you admire most in the story?
- Give your feelings about Angeline at the end of the story.
- Which character would you like to have with you on a survival mission? (5 to 7 minutes)

SECOND READING
(Focus on reflection, considered response, rhetorical/story values, emergent issues and themes)

Using angles or points raised by students' first responses, the teacher directs students back for a closer look at selected sections of the story. With basic-narrative and early enriched-story readers (a typical grade six or seven class), the questions below would not be shown to students; rather they form a blueprint for the teacher's lesson plan on this part of the story. More experienced classes could do some of this work in small-group discussion, with the questions on an overhead transparency. In either case, reflective time — at seats, in groups, at home — is essential. Question 3 is optional, to be used if the teacher wishes to introduce, and the students are ready for, a second theme (the demands of the larger unit might determine the choices here).

Introduction and Body (to p. 38, par. 2)
1. At the beginning of the adventure, some doubts are raised about whether Angeline should accompany the three boys.
(a) Who has the strongest objections? The least? Why?

(b) What feelings or attitudes does each of the boys show towards Angeline? How did *she* feel?
(c) At this point in the story, what were *your* feelings on the matter? For example, was she right or just foolish?
2.(a) Comment on how well Angeline copes with each of these 'trials' during the trip. Give specific details to support your assessment.
• shooting the rapids on the first day (pp. 30–31)
• the attack of the black flies
• the canoe-tipping episode (pp. 38–39)
(b) What qualities of character does she show throughout?
(c) How typical or exceptional do these seem to you?
3. The boys come from different cultures: white, Cree and Innuit.
(a) Compare and contrast these differences by looking at the opinions, feelings and reactions they have in regard to:
• the world of nature (the river, the flies, the trees and rocks)
• the wolves
• the sense of time (bottom of p. 34)
(b) What is Jamie learning about the Cree and Innuit culture (way-of-life) as the adventure continues?

THIRD READING
(Focus on moral-thematic response, reflection and discussion; connections with life, books, self and society)

The continuing interpretation of the story and its emerging themes moves into a more reflective, student-centred, open-ended phase. The teacher initiates the questions, adapting them to the particular slant and focus of the students' efforts during second reading, and arranges appropriate discussion formats (small-group to whole-class, whole-class introduction followed by small-group discussion and whole-class take-up, etc.). During any summary discussions the teacher takes the role of chairperson only. Sections of questions marked with an asterisk may be used as reflective journal prompts.

The Conclusion (p. 39 to the end) and the Story-as-a-Whole:
4. During the episode with the lost rifle (pp. 39–42) Angeline not only proves to be the equal of the boys, she demonstrates special qualities and skills that combine to save the day.

(a) Show to what extent this statement is true by referring to details from the episode.
(b) What special feelings are shown by Awasin, Jamie and Peetyuk before, during and after Angeline's dive? Who do you think appreciates her the most? Give reasons.
(c) To what degree are the attitudes that each of the boys showed at the beginning of the story changed or confirmed by Angeline's action? Who was the most surprised? Why?
(d) To what degree is Jamie typical of how Canadian society views women? Give your opinion.*
5. While Jamie is a proud and sometimes bold leader, he has many things to learn about the North and the native way of life.
(a) Illustrate his leadership role by referring to at least three statements or actions he makes in different parts of the story.
(b) At what points does he need the expert advice of Awasin and Peetyuk? Give examples. How well does he receive and use this advice?
(c) In doing so, how much and how deeply does he learn about native customs, values and attitudes? How much did *you* learn?*
(d) Whom did you admire most in the story? Why?*

THIRD-READING EXTENSION
(Follow-up writing)

Not every individual story or text studied in class will lead to or merit a reflective-summarizing response in writing from each student. The study of short stories within a unit, however, provides many natural opportunities for follow-up writing. At other times, summarizing response will best be served by small-group discussion and/or the various journal entries accumulated, and subsequently read by the teacher. The three options given below provide differentiated tasks tailored to the reading stage, experience, and ability level of students.[14] More advanced readers, it must be remembered, can profit not only from the more cognitively demanding essay format, but also from lots of expressive and poetic tasks. One type of task does not exclude another; nor do advanced readers outgrow the particular pleasures and uses of the expressive and poetic.

1. In your literature journal, write about (a) some sort of prejudice you have experienced or observed, or (b) some insight you've recently had into how other people (different from you) behave.
[Expressive mode, for print-shy or basic-narrative readers]

2. Write a one-to-two-page story representing a further adventure on the Big River. Use the first-person "I"; select one of the characters from the original story; try to see and describe things through his or her viewpoint.
[Narrative-descriptive mode, transposed story-incident, for experienced basic-narrative or enriched-story readers]

3. Choose one of the statements below and, using it as a guide, write a commentary (about three-quarters of a page) in which you show to what extent you believe it to be a fair comment on the story. Use details from the story and from your own experience to support your views. You may use the first person.

(a) While he still has much to learn about human behaviour and life in the North, Jamie proves to be a bold, courageous and resourceful leader though his own character flaws occasionally direct the group towards disaster.

(b) The native characters in the story — Angeline, Peetyuk and Awasin — display virtues and skills that allow them to be survivors in a harsh land, but it is Jamie's special qualities that make him the natural leader.

(c) Though Angeline, time and again, proves herself to be equal and sometimes superior to the boys in the story, to some degree they do not recognize her qualities.
[First-person commentary, essay-format, for enriched-story or gifted readers]

Resources

The titles listed below have been selected because they are consistent with the theory and pedagogical principles outlined above. I have emphasized materials that illustrate second and third reading because they are the most problematic aspects of teaching fiction aesthetically.

Johan Aitken, "Myth, Legend and Fairy Tale: 'Serious Statements About Our Existence,'" in *Growing With Books*, Book I (Toronto: Ontario Ministry of Education, 1988). An excellent rationale for including these now-controversial genres in grades one to six, with clear directions about how to teach them.

Michael Benton and Geoff Fox, *Teaching Literature: Nine to Fourteen* (Oxford: Oxford University Press, 1985). Some helpful strategies for thinking about teaching the novel in grades four to nine, but many of the extension activities drift perilously close to the reading-by-doing fallacy. Use of the response-journal and other forms of expressive writing are well illustrated.

Casebooks in Canadian Literature, 5 vols. (Toronto: McClelland and Stewart, 1978–1979). While limited to Canadian writers, the general strength of this series lies in its third-reading questions and extensions on a thematic unit of short stories; on its comparative questions and assignments on the short stories, three related novels, and counterpoints (quotations from the authors, critics, et al.); on its developmental, second-reading question sets on the three novels; and on suggestions for independent study projects that emerge from both aesthetic and thematic reading. The related novels for each title are given in parentheses:

Jim French, *Journeys I* (Paperny, *The Wooden People*; Mowat, *Lost in the Barrens*; Harris, *Raven's Cry*): gr. 7–8.

Jim French, *Journeys II* (Bodsworth, *The Last of the Curlews*; Epps, *The Outlaw of the Megantic*; Roberts, *The Red Feathers*): gr. 9–10.

Don Gutteridge, *Mountain and Plain* (Roy, *Where Nests the Water Hen*; Ross, *As For Me and My House*; Buckler, *The Mountain and the Valley*): gr. 12.

———, Rites of Passage (MacLennan, *Barometer Rising*; Laurence, *A Jest of God*; Ostenso, *Wild Geese*): gr. 12.

Ian Underhill, *Family Portraits* (Laurence, *A Bird in the House*; Callaghan, *They Shall Inherit the Earth*; Richler, *Son of a Smaller Hero*): gr. 12.

Pat Cleator, Eleanor McRoberts and Don Gutteridge, *Rhetoric: A Unified Approach to English Curricula* (Toronto: OISE Press, 1970). The section on the elementary school contains three integrated language arts units for grades four to seven involving fiction, legends, poetry, and a variety of poetry-writing activities.

Geoffrey Eggins, *Learning Through Talking: 11–16* (London: Evans/Methuen, 1979). An indispensable book on why and how to use small-group discussion in the teaching of literature, with practical advice and illustration. While not directly aesthetic — the roots of the U.K. talking pedagogy lie in the expressive theories of James Britton — the methods here are readily transferable to many aspects of first and second reading.

Don Gutteridge, *Brave Season: Reading and the Language Arts in Grades Seven to Ten* (London, ON: The Althouse Press, 1983). Contains a fully developed theory of growth in reading, the role of questions, a rationale for first, second and third reading, practical examples of literature theme-units (with novels, stories and poems), and aesthetic-driven extension activities. The first-reading concept is weakened, however, by the absence of the student response journal and its various uses.

Don Gutteridge with James French and Carol Keyes Deimling, *The Country of the Young: Units in Canadian Literature for Elementary and Secondary School* (London, ON: The Althouse Press, 1978). Presents teachers with a variety of detailed units — integrated, generic and thematic — with fiction and poetry at the centre. Novels treated intensively include Montgomery, *Anne of Green Gables*; Munro, *Lives of Girls and Women*; Richter, *The Light in the Forest*; Aubry, *Agouhanna*; and Buchan, *Copper Sunrise*.

Don Gutteridge, Incredible Journeys, New Approaches to the Novel: A Handbook for Teachers, rev. ed. (London, ON: The Althouse Press, 1990). The revised edition outlines a number of uses for the student-response journal, along with explicit instructions for teaching the core and complementary novel in grades seven to ten, and two complete study guides: one on Hubert's *Dreamspeaker* and one on *The Diary of Anne Frank*. Appendix C contains a four-stage developmental model for reading fiction.

———, "A Unit in Indian Mythology for Grade Seven," *Classmate* II, 1 (Feb. 1973), 23–32. An integrated unit using film and orally presented myths and legends from the Glooscap cycle, culminating in student-written myths.

Cornelia Hoogland, "Poetics, Politics and Pedagogy of Grimm's Fairy Tales" (PhD diss., Simon Fraser University, 1993). A rationale for teaching fairy tales, with several detailed lessons as illustration.

David Jackson, *Encounters With Books: Teaching Fiction 11–16* (London: Methuen, 1983). A pioneering effort in response-centred teaching of the novel, underpinned by a strong, workable sense of stages of growth. Specific novels are treated and student response well illustrated. The practical pedagogy here should be set against the more developed and theoretical framework laid out in Jackson's *Continuity in Secondary English* (London: Methuen, 1982), which covers the whole of junior and senior high school. The stage theory for the language arts at the end of the book is the most detailed and sensible one extant.

Jean and Ian Malloch, *Literature Alive*, 4 vols. (Mississauga, ON: S.B.F. Media, 1990). A series of kits and teacher handbooks for units of literature and extension activities centred on the whole-class study of a novel. Each volume, two for grade seven and two for grade eight, focusses on three or four novels. Guides are complete with daybook outline, group-discussion questions and follow-up activities, the latter being very much aesthetic-driven. The fact that each student does not have a copy of the novel under study, though easily rectified, is an inherent weakness of the programme design. For a detailed account of one teacher's experience with the Malloch approach and materials, see Margaret Klementowicz, "Literature as Shared Experience: A Study of the *Literature Alive* Programme," (MEd, University of Western Ontario, 1993).

Joy F. Moss, *Focus Units in Literature: A Handbook for Elementary School Teachers* (Urbana, IL: NCTE, 1984). A rationale, with examples, of a whole-class approach to novels, with both generic and thematic emphasis. Best suited to grades four to six and to advanced, enriched-story readers.

Robert Protherough, *Developing Response to Fiction* (Milton Keynes, UK: Open University Press, 1983). The rationale and stage theory are superb and would serve as a preface to any English programme based on literature and aesthetic response and expression. The authored contributions serving as illustration, alas, do not always accurately represent Protherough's own balanced and sensible theory, and should therefore be approached with caution.

Albert Somers and Janet Worthington, *Response Guides For Teaching Children's Books* (Urbana, IL: NCTE, 1979). An invaluable series of discussion questions on novels and storybooks from grades one to eight, with excellent extension activities into the related arts. The question sets are best suited to grades four to six (in fact, are a model for these grades), but all are aesthetically sound. Among the twenty-seven titles included are classics like *Where the Wild Things Are, Charlotte's Web, Sounder, Old Yeller* and *A Wrinkle in Time.*

Study-Guides on the Core Novel, New Approaches to the Novel, 33 vols., Don Gutteridge, general editor (London, ON: The Althouse Press, 1986, 1990, 1992). An ongoing series of question sets and extension activities on novels for grades six to twelve. Includes both classics and contemporary young-adult titles, aesthetic-based and keyed to the handbook, *Incredible Journeys.*

Ian Underhill, *Starting the Ark in the Dark: Teaching Canadian Literature in High School* (London, ON: The Althouse Press, 1977). Illustrates how novels, short stories and poems can be studied with aesthetic and generic integrity and then extended to third- and fourth-reading activities; in particular, the cultural context of literature as seen from its regional roots and its social and artistic setting therein. Lots of group discussion and student-initiated independent-project work.

4

Poetic Writing

Poetic and Expressive

An understanding of aesthetic reading that includes why and how poems and stories are composed makes it possible to define the nature of poetic writing with clarity and pedagogical import. Thirty years ago in the heyday of what was then called the "creative writing movement,"[1] no one would have asked for such a definition. Students from kindergarten to grade twelve were sat down before National Film Board films, coloured slides and recordings of music or professionally recited poetry, and simply invited to express themselves in story or verse.[2] And did so, apparently, with enthusiasm and vigour.[3] It was the pioneering research of James Britton and associates in the early 1970s that clarified for teachers, whose creative excitement was occasionally less than focussed, the various kinds of writing promoted in schools.[4] While Britton's categories stabilized definitions of the modes of writing for a time, they inadvertently prepared the ground for future confusions.

It was during these years that the terms "expressive," "transactional" and "poetic" entered the lexicon, and soon made their way into curriculum guidelines, conference speeches and professional workshops. While these three categories were, as it turned out, conceptually muddled from the beginning, they were clear enough to bring a new category into focus and prominence. Teachers had a general idea of what they thought was meant by poetic, and transactional seemed to be just another way of describing expository and argumentative writing. But what on earth was this "expressive" mode? Britton defined it thus:[5]

Expressive Writing	
Features	*Formats*
(1) The writer is the first-person "I"	• the friendly letter (the median type)
(2) "I" writes to a known audience, the second-person "you"	
(3) "I" expresses the "self" — its views, feelings its understanding of a topic, etc. — to a sympathetic, friendly audience	• diary and personal journal (private)
(4) Which results in a loose coherence, an associative or narrative flow, and a speech-like tone, syntax and diction	• opinion/response journal, reading log (semi-public, read by teacher)

Many teachers at that time assumed that the "written-down speech" produced by those students of theirs who had read little and were relegated to general or non-academic classes was really the symptom of weak language skills and, hence, a type of writing to be eradicated, not encouraged. Nonetheless, Britton and others soon succeeded in convincing progressive teachers to accept the expressive as a discrete, embryonic mode of writing with some developmental features of its own and with the potential, under the right conditions, to evolve into the more formal and discursive modes required in the senior years of schooling: the note, the essay, the written components of projects, and so on. Britton's initial error lay in his claim that the kind of expressive writing to be found in the friendly letter or casual journal entry would develop, more or less as a function of maturation, into the poetic mode as well; that is, into poems, fiction (stories, narrative incidents), fables, myths, legends and drama scripts.

The analysis of aesthetic reading in chapters 1 to 3 helps to explain why expressive forms can *under no circumstances* be pressed to turn into poetic ones. Poems and stories are composed by *projection*, not expression. The poet, working initially with only a half-conscious sense of where the words, images, rhythms and emerging shape of the poem are taking him, allows his unarticulated feeling-thought to *become* the poem and its words (the text). Even the presence of a first-person persona in a poem (or story) is fictional, that is, the writer takes up some temporary role pertinent only to the poem's context. After a poem has been "closed" and frozen in print, the author becomes just another reader, albeit one with a vested interest in what the poem is saying back to its creator. When young student-writers are unable to project their feelings into the words of a poem or story, or they use a first-person narrator as a simple extension of themselves, then what they produce will be expressive, not poetic. Here we have, then, an absolutely discriminating criterion for defining the two modes.

Below is a student's poem — composed in a single, unrevised effort — that illustrates the principles of projected emotion, writing in role, and the marriage of form and feeling.

Roses

One day I woke up
And I looked out my window
And there were roses all around,
Pink ones and red ones,
I went out and felt them and feeled them,
And they were nice and soft
Like my sister's velvet dress,
And they smelled like a birthday cake
And like I would be in the woods
When I am walking.

Jason

In Jason's poem, the "I" is a persona, as it is in the most accomplished love lyric by John Donne or Leonard Cohen, the self projected into a drama he narrates, depicts and participates in. The childlike "feeled them and feeled them" embodies for the reader the innocence of the voice and its profoundly simple pleasures: "felt them and felt them" would be anomalous here, rhythmically flat and repetitively banal. The interacting effects of the similes, the rhythmic exactness of line length, the nicely ungrammatical "like I would be" to set up the final analogy, and the lilting anapests of "in the woods / When I am walking", all these carry and buttress the dominant feeling-thought. This is, of course, an exceptional poem, one that was singled out by Jason's teachers for inclusion in a city-wide, published anthology.[6] Jason himself must have been pleased, especially because he was only in grade one at the time, and could not yet print his name; the poem was dictated to his teacher, who typed as he recited.

The chart below summarizes the nature of the poetic mode.

Expressive Writing

Features

(1) The "self" is projected into the form (language, structure, persona); use of "I" will be in role

(2) Through projection the writer conveys feeling, thought, attitude (i.e., through the detail of the poem or story)

(3) Coherence or closure follow the conventions of the format as understood tacitly by the writer, and are produced under strong stimulus and without explicit or conscious control

(4) The writer has no immediate sense of audience; after the fact, the audience is a public one: teacher as kind expert, the class as sympathetic responders

Formats

- *prose fiction*: myth, legend, fairy tale, pattern-story, narrative incident, short story
- *verse*: pattern poems (haiku, cinquain, acrostic); open form (free verse); closed form (rhyming stanzas, ballad, sonnet, etc.)
- *drama scripts*: dramatizations from given texts; original scenes, full-length scripts

---

Keeping poetic and expressive modes discrete and clear in our minds is critical to developing a writing programme in the grades below ten; that is, before the sophisticated prose rhythm, logical substructure, and increasingly abstract vocabulary of discursive forms are available to students, and even then only to those who can be persuaded to read widely in them (e.g., essays, textbooks, magazines, pamphlets and reports). As we have seen, most middle-school students have limited or no tacit knowledge of the argumentative/expository formats of the discursive because they have not been exposed to them or taken them up. Such formats, despite our quixotic efforts to force-feed them to students, are late-developing forms of writing. Without a wide and deep reading base, their "grammar" cannot be internalized, and no one anywhere has yet been able to convince young readers to abandon the delights of story and verse for the intellectual rigour of argument and the formal essay.

What this means for teaching, then, is that below grade ten, the writing curriculum will have to rely almost exclusively on expressive and poetic writing forms. Understanding the unique nature and purpose of each of the latter and their particular educational uses will be necessary, and productive. As we have already seen, students' tacit knowledge of story and verse — unlike discursive forms — is early in development, deeply internalized and amenable to constant growth in pedagogically nurturing circumstances. That is why poetry and fiction that is well beyond the independent reading ability of students can be introduced and studied under the guidance of a teacher. We teach not only what students can see, but much that they can merely sense.

In similar fashion, expressive writing is readily prompted as soon as students can print their letters because, as Britton has shown, it is a written extension of speech and the associative rhythm. If students can talk, they can express that talk in written form, especially if they feel that their audience is a teacher who will receive it uncritically (in the conventional sense) and write back in kind. Expressive writing has also been successful in the primary grades as an invaluable aid to emergent reading. And right across the K-to-12 curriculum, the promotion of the various uses of the journal — a basic school format for expressive writing — has been one of the most important advances in pedagogy in the past forty years.[7] In English class, from grade four onward, its uses are vital and irreplaceable:

Pedagogical Uses of Expressive Writing

Use	*Format*
• improvement of fluency and confidence	• daily personal journal
• immediate or reflective response to literature	• literature journal, response journal, reading log
• comfortable expository tasks (first-person commentary on literature)	• literature notebook
• transposed expressive writing, prompted from stories, novels, etc.	• "pretend" letter, journal, diary; student writes in role of character from a story, novel, etc.

Unfortunately, the enthusiasm with which many teachers took up the expressive journal and adopted many of the methods loosely associated with it, like group discussion and collaborative talk, has led to a corresponding depreciation of poetic writing. The two modes are, of course, distinct in form, use and effect. Not only are they not mutually exclusive in the classroom, they are equally necessary to the overall development of writing abilities, and invaluable as aids to both aesthetic and other kinds of reading. A glance at the following chart will indicate the unique uses of poetic writing.

Pedagogical Uses of Poetic Writing

Use	*Format*
• extension of thought and feeling through *projected* language and form; unity, coherence and closure are learned here as *powerful linguistic processes*	• stories, poems, myths, legends, fairy tales, drama and radio scripts
• connections between literature and students' own efforts in kind are externalized and reinforced	

- fluency of prose sentences (syntax and rhetoric) and connotative diction
- tone, voice and writing in role

The reciprocity to be achieved between the aesthetic-reading components of an English course and the poetic-writing ones are as obvious as they are numerous, but will only be effective as long as poems and stories are prompted by initially powerful stimuli, and students are encouraged to experience the first-draft rush of authentic poetic writing. Moreover, because such first drafts are, even with professional writers, about 90 percent complete, follow-up revision and drafting will necessarily be limited. With younger students it will be of dubious value in any circumstance. Keep in mind also that open-form poetry, literature-prompted story-incidents, and interesting transposition tasks (writing in role from a story studied) are the most "natural" formats for inducing engaged and projected texts from students of all ages. On the other hand, closed forms like the sonnet and ballad, the full-length short story, and the novel are sophisticated formats, ones that students enjoy reading but find almost impossible to write from the inside out, simply because they will expend almost all of their energy in rhyme hunting or casting about for enough material and rhetorical ballast to carry them through to closure. The danger here, besides students' inevitable frustration, is that much of the patient work done by the teacher in literature class — to convince students of the happy ambiguity and gestalt-like leaps of insight intrinsic to aesthetic interpretation — may be undone. For once students get into their heads the notion that poems and stories are patched together from the outside in, and that the whole is the simple sum of those explicitly-stitched fragments, then the aesthetic game is up — and over. If aesthetic reading is to be successfully taught and developed, authentic poetic-writing tasks will have to be made an integral part of English from kindergarten to grade twelve. Put another way, just because the essay or independent study project become important and *do*able by grade twelve does not mean that writing poems, brief fictional pieces, and transposed texts arising out of aspects of literature study should be curtailed. By the same token, the value of entries in students' response-journals during a first reading of *Hamlet* or *Wuthering Heights* does not diminish just because grade twelves are capable of carrying out second-reading analyses.

Poetic Writing: Some Practical Suggestions

Much of the poetic writing in English class will arise out of aspects of the aesthetic reading and extension of poems, short stories and novels, simply because an immersion in a unit of poems, for example, is the ideal setting in which to have students write their own. Both form and motive will be near to hand. However, the use of a short film or a five-minute tape of short poems on a current theme or type of poem should not be overlooked as immediate stimuli. Here is an outline of procedures that have proved effective from grades four to twelve, and which I have labelled HSQR (high stimulus/quick response).[8]

> (1) Following the whole-class study of a short story or a unit of lyric poems, prepare a four-to-six-minute audiotape of short poems that reflect the feeling, theme, topic, or character(s) just studied and discussed. Draw upon professional sources or fellow teachers to provide the oral presentation of the material. Optionally, a seven-to-ten-minute film on a similar topic may be used in addition to the audiotape.
>
> (2) Play the tape once, and have students jot down, in column A of a blank sheet of paper, adjectives or phrases to describe their feelings as they listen. In a brisk three-minute take-up, record student responses on the blackboard, without comment. Similar responses may be grouped there to illustrate to students the focussed power of poetry.
>
> (3) Play the tape again and ask students to write down, in column B and *as they listen*, any phrases or lines that they find interesting. In a brisk five-minute take-up, phrases are recorded on the blackboard exactly as they are given by students; repeated ones are highlighted (again, that focussed power) and variants noted (but not corrected).
>
> (4) Play the tape a third time, and tell students to relax, listen and (i) add to or complete phrases in column B and/or (ii) begin to write a poem — a quick first-draft only — on the general topic of the sequence (e.g., old age, winter contrasts, sadness, nature, childhood, imagination, spring and fall, love). Students may borrow images, ideas or words from the poems on the tape. Their first draft should be

written on a blank, unruled sheet of paper and completed in no more than five minutes, with follow-up revision and rewriting later on, as needed.
(5) Optionally, a short film related to the topic may be run as soon as the tape is finished, after which students begin to write, immediately and with no discussion. (Talk will kill the first-draft rush.)

As noted earlier, the full-length short story and novel are risky options as poetic-writing tasks. Units of short stories and the intensive whole-class study of a novel do, however, provide excellent opportunities for a variety of fictional efforts by students. Below are two sets of such tasks from which the teacher or the student may select the one most appropriate, following a thorough reading of the text. One set is suitable for grade six or seven (based on *The Secret Garden*) and one for grade eleven or twelve (based on *Huckleberry Finn*). Of special significance is the use of transposed point of view (recasting powerful scenes from the original narrative viewpoint to a new one), rewritten incidents, students' own extension of an incident (not a whole story or new chapter), and various in-role tasks in relaxed expressive formats like the "pretend" journal or friendly letter. Despite their expressive format, the latter are poetic because the student-writer is still projecting the self into an imagined character and circumstance.

Moreover, there is double value in having students write poetically out of their literature study: the assessment of their achievement may be judged in part by the content (how well the particular section of the novel was understood and transposed) and in part by the language and rhetoric of the piece itself (e.g., a well-told incident, or a letter whose style reflects the chosen character and situation).

Finally, the variety of formats suggested in each set is meant to offer teachers and students much more than mere choice. They provide a range of levels of difficulty: writing an additional, original narrative incident is a more complex rhetorical and imaginative task than penning a friendly letter in role, where much of the detail and most of the character's personality is already known. What teachers need, especially in the middle-school transition years, is to be able to select on behalf of individual students, or nudge them towards, poetic-writing assignments that they can handle successfully. An important bonus is the fact that, in the absence of suitable essay formats, many transposition tasks, in conjunction with reflective journal entries, may be used to help assess students' deep understanding of a core story or novel.

THE SECRET GARDEN[9]

1. Choose one of the following:

(a) Pretend that you are Martha and that you are writing a letter to your mother and the whole Sowerby family. Tell all about your new mistress, Mary. Describe how she looks and acts; discuss her background in India; tell how you feel and what you think about her treatment of you and Mrs. Medlock.

(b) Pretend that you are Mary, and write several diary entries describing:
- the cholera epidemic in India
- the trip to Misselthwaite Manor
- your first encounter with Mrs. Medlock and with Martha

2. Choose one of the following:

(a) Imagine that you are the robin. Describe your bird's-eye view of the secret garden:
- just before Mary sees it for the first time
- just before Colin sees it for the first time

(b) Imagine that you are Dickon. From Dickon's point of view (use the first person "I"), describe your first meeting with Mary. Be sure to include what you see and feel when you and Mary go into the garden together for the first time.

3. Choose one of the following:

(a) Draw or paint a picture of how you think the secret garden looks in full bloom.

(b) Write a poem or a prose description of the secret garden. Find pictures of gardens or flowers to illustrate your poem or description.

4. Imagine that Colin and Dickon have grown up. Choose one of the following:

(a) You are Dickon, and you have gone to London to study to become a veterinarian. Write a letter to Mary describing how you came to love and understand animals so well.

(b) You are Colin, now married with a ten-year-old daughter. Write a letter to her in which you tell about Mary and the effect that she had on your life.

HUCKLEBERRY FINN[10]

1. Select one of the following; pay particular attention to the use of dialect:

(a) Write a journal, from Jim's point of view, covering any four days between the time Huck escaped from Pap and the time Huck arrived at the Phelps' farm.

(b) Write a journal account of the "rescue" from Tom's point of view.

2. To what extent do you think Huck will carry out his resolution at the end of the novel to "light out for the territory ahead of the rest"?
Write your version of chapter 44. Include one or two major events, and try to capture Huck's feelings and experiences in his own words.

3. Based on what you think might happen after chapter 43, choose one of the following:

(a) Write a dialogue between Tom and Jim that could occur the next morning; be true to their viewpoints and dialects, and indicate what course of action they will decide to pursue.

(b) Write a dialogue between Aunt Sally and Uncle Silas that indicates their reaction to Huck's plan.

4. With a partner or your group write a brief radio script (with sound cues, voice-over narration, etc.) based on one of the following scenes:
   - chapters 6–7: Huck's captivity with Pap and his escape
   - chapters 19–20: rescuing the duke and the king and the Parkville pirate sermon
   - chapters 21–22: the Colonel Sherburn incident
   - chapters 29–30: the testing of the king and the duke, and their escape
   - chapters 36–39: the preparations for the rescue

   Dramatize your scene on audiotape, and play it for the class.

5. Do one of the following:

   (a) Write a letter from Aunt Polly to a friend of hers in a nearby town, in which she describes the attempts of the Widow Douglas and Miss Watson to educate Huck.

   (b) Write a series of three or four diary entries that the king or the duke might have made after the success of one of their scams. (This could also be an extended single entry.)

6. Huck is now grown up; he returns from "the territory" to visit St. Petersburg. Write a dialogue, one-to-two pages in length, between Huck and one of the following:
   - Widow Douglas
   - Aunt Polly
   - Tom
   - Jim
   - the king and the duke

There are, of course, many other ways to stimulate student writing in the poetic mode, including the time-honoured use of music and short films as prompts, and a host of drama-based activities. Whatever the nature of the stimulus, however, the critical features of poetic writing remain the same: it must be projected from the student's emotions and feelings into the detail of the text, must be "in role" one way or another, must be intentionally public (that is, any "frozen" text may be read by unknown others), and ought to emerge, under optimum conditions, with a characteristic first-draft rush. Like aesthetic reading, poetic writing calls for a pedagogy specifically shaped to its inimitable nature and purpose.

Resources

Some of the items below are devoted mainly to prompting students to write poems, stories, legends, etc., but others illustrate the role of poetic writing in integrated language arts units. Many of the titles are more than thirty years old, but that is because the heyday of creative writing in schools occurred during the 1960s. Other resources involving integrated units that include poetic writing may be found in the resource section for fiction in chapter 3.

Jack Beckett, *The Keen Edge: An Analysis of Poems by Adolescents* (London: Blackie and Son, 1965). A practical guide for encouraging student poetry writing and learning what to say about it. Contains 100 pages of students' poems.

Jack Cameron and Emma Plattor, *The Leaf Not the Tree: Teaching Poetry Through Film and Tape* (Toronto: Gage, 1971). Innovative handbook and kit for teachers of creative writing in elementary and high school.

Ronald L. Cramer, *Children's Writing and Language Growth* (Columbus, OH: Merrill, 1978). A straightforward handbook on teaching various kinds of writing in school, including the poetic. A common-sense primer for beginning teachers.

Robert Druce, *The Eye of Innocence: Children and Their Poetry* (Leicester: Brockhampton Press, 1965). Argues for the value of poetry and the precision of language it promotes. Contains sound ideas for stimulating verse in class and practical suggestions for helping students revise and polish their first drafts.

Barbara Juster Esbensen, *A Celebration of Bees: Helping Children Write Poetry* (Minneapolis: Winston, 1975). An excellent practical book for elementary school teachers.

Don Gutteridge, *The Dimension of Delight: A Study of Children's Verse Writing, Ages 11-13*, Research Studies in Education 3 (London, ON: The Althouse Press, 1988). Provides an introduction to expressive and poetic modes of writing, defines and illustrates five subcategories of naive verse (the kind that students write), and analyzes more than 500 poems produced by students in grades six to eight.

David Holbrook, *The Secret Places* (London: Cambridge University Press, 1964). An inspiring book about the value of poetry and poetic writing to middle-school students, with case studies and many poignant examples.

Marjorie L. Hourd, *The Education of the Poetic Spirit* (London: Heinemann, 1949, repr. 1968). The book that launched two decades of creative writing fervour: a passionate defense of the aesthetic in the lives of children.

Dan Kirby and Tom Liner, *Inside Out: Developmental Strategies for Teaching Writing* (Upper Montclair, NJ: Boynton/Cook, 1983). A practical handbook, short on consistent theory (they try to merge vague process assumptions with their own strong sense of form and aesthetics), but otherwise very useful. Chapter 6 on poetry writing is excellent.

Kenneth Koch, *Wishes, Lies and Dreams: Teaching Children to Write Poetry* (New York: Chelsea House, 1970). An American classic on the free-spirited, prompted writing of poems by children in school. Includes dozens of students' poems and pedagogical comment on them. Particularly strong on the use of stimuli and starters.

Denys Thompson, *Children As Poets* (London: Heinemann, 1972). An inspiring anthology of poems written by students aged five to eighteen, with an excellent postscript on the nature and value of poetry in the classroom.

5

Sound Theory / Good Practice

Theory Gone Awry: the Case of Writing Process

The creative writing movement was the *Zeitgeist* of the English curriculum in North America and the United Kingdom during the hectic sixties and early seventies. While the claims it made for improving the psychological health of children and putting them in touch with the better parts of the human spirit were doubtless more enthusiastic than realistic, they gave rise to a number of new teaching methods that survived long after the movement itself waned. The use of films,[1] recordings, photographs and paintings to stimulate "free writing" helped make these exotic instruments familiar to the book-and-blackboard set and, English teachers being what they are, they soon found other ways to incorporate technology into their classrooms. The role of professionally presented poetry, fiction and Shakespearean drama on recording and audiotape (and, later, on videotape) in strengthening the methodology of first reading cannot be overestimated. With the introduction and widespread use of the journal in the late seventies and early eighties, and the expressive mode of writing it helped legitimate, first reading was able to be integrated fully into an aesthetic-based literature curriculum. Which is to say that both kinds of writing supportive of aesthetic reading — expressive and poetic — were recognized, were accessible to all students (because of internalized tacit knowledge), and were teachable because the methodology was understood and had been validated through practice. By the mid-eighties, then, we ought to have been witness to the consolidation and dissemination of a viable, proven pedagogy for English studies.

This did not happen for a number of reasons,[2] one of which concerns us directly: the productive use of the expressive and the poetic was sideswiped by the untimely arrival of a pedagogy called, by its progenitors, Writing Process (WP). I have elsewhere dissected the theory and practice of WP,[3] but suffice it to say here that the methodology first propounded by Donald Graves and widely promulgated by Lucy Calkins is an object lesson and cautionary tale, wherein flawed theory generates specious practice. The theory, which has to be inferred because none of its adherents has yet iterated it in continuous prose, appears to be based on two bold assumptions: (1) that children as young as seven years of age can be systematically and explicitly taught to manipulate metacognitive understandings in order to produce and revise their writing in school, and (2) that there is a single, describable cognitive process for the production and revision of all forms of written expression. Since neither of these is supportable in light of competing and mutually exclusive sets of assumptions, and since neither has been shown to work in practice, the results in actual classrooms are sadly predictable.

First, the process of metacognition is not particularly stable when it refers to the idea of knowing how you know and hence being able to consciously manipulate your knowing. But even if we take the concept at face value, in the poetic mode of composing, as we have seen, very little is consciously known or fully grasped at the point of utterance. And this is because the most effective poems, of mature or naive writers, are the outcome of tacit processes and understandings. Despite the claims to the contrary of some contemporary writers, it is only during the revision stage that professional poets become intellectually aware of what they are reading back to themselves when they pause to get some idea of where the first draft has been taking them. Even so, we have compelling testimony from all kinds of imaginative writers that they cannot, even years into their career, recount the precise steps they take to revise a line or adjust a metaphor. If mature and successful writers have not taken pains to become metacognitively aware, then why should nine-year-old tyros penning their first poem? Of course, seasoned writers do have a developed metacognitive sense of what constitutes for them a completed and satisfactory poem, but for most of them it is still kept in the zone of tacit awareness, just below consciousness. Moreover, veteran writers are also veteran *readers*, in which role they can step back and critique their own drafts within some framework of cognitive and affective criteria, what we usually call sensibility. Surely this is why they so often say, in trying to explain a particular revision, "It *sounds* better like this." The main point here is that student-writers will only be able to revise their poems in the manner of veterans when they have read as widely. *Revision in poetic writing, then, is governed by the extent and sophistication of the reading-base.*

Nonetheless, Writing Process gained our attention because Graves, Calkins and others were able to demonstrate that grade-four students *could* be put through a series of hoops — jump by jump — in composing "personal narratives," that drafting protocols could be demonstrated and mimicked, and that the final draft, if not unequivocally superior, was always well worked over and scrubbed up. The use of peers as the budding author's initial audience and feedback mechanism pleased everyone who wished to promote collaborative learning and social cohesion. For many teachers, particularly those in elementary schools,[4] WP offered, for the first time, a step-by-step, manageable method of organizing a writing component in English classes.

The claim, however, that by externalizing all parts of the composing process and learning to self-manage the drafting protocols, students were truly gaining an understanding of them and were deploying them metacognitively to monitor and adjust their own productions was never supported by credible evidence. In order to justify such an assertion, it would have to be shown that students progressively internalized the stages of the process and, as they did so, needed less and less to replicate them consciously, and, further, that the more sophisticated variants of the process required for discursive forms like argument would be subsequently added and incorporated. That is what we all do when we learn anything: to read, write or ride a bicycle. We internalize as many of the moves as we can in order to perform them more and more automatically, leaving room for conscious attention to overarching goals like doing wheelies. In fact, the so-called cognitive moves of WP have always been *operational procedures*, not true forms of cognitive processing. Remembering to number your drafts, to read aloud each set of changes to your support-group of peers and keep only those emendations that visibly "work" on the group, to revisit the *personal* (actual) experience that originally motivated the piece as a source of fresh data, and to conference each term with your teacher to determine in tandem where you are as a writer and where you have to go — these may be useful moves for writers to adopt in general, but they are not cognitive in nature. Hence, they are not learned cognitively, but rather are apprehended by dogged imitation and rote practice.

In addition to this confusing conflation of procedural and cognitive processes, WP has also induced many teachers to accept the claim that its process (even if it were cognitive and metacognitive) is the way in which all written composition is produced. But as Calkins herself has admitted,[5] the most dedicated attempts to use WP procedures to persuade students to write poems and stories of real value — ones that show development and maturation over time — have been disappointing. Once again, the basic assumptions about composition were flawed. As we have seen in chapter 4, Britton's findings and the successful implementation of them in classrooms here and abroad had already suggested that the expressive and poetic modes were discrete in function, in their composing process, in formal structure, and in the adjustments made to them by audiences or readers.

Unfortunately, WP relied almost exclusively upon one format to demonstrate the workability of its lock-step procedures: the personal narrative. Personal-narrative, in the narrow sense used by Graves and Calkins, is in truth a spruced-up variant of "What I Did on My Summer Holidays," because it is invariably written in the first person, that person is the author (not a persona), and the events are supposed to be drawn from the writer's own personal experience. The format is nominally the story, but it is story in its narrowest sense: the chronological arrangement of events told by the author to a nearby audience: the ever-hovering peer-review group or conferencing teacher. In other words, WP personal-narrative starts life in a format close to the conversational anecdote. Descriptive language and fresh events are added and reworked, on the advice of peer reviewers, to make the account appear more like a short story. But none of these revisions alters the underlying rhetorical structure: a bare-bones narrative constrained by an unprojected "I."

Besides being a hugely time-consuming pedagogy — workshopping, elaborate conferencing, obsessive record-keeping — with no record of progress made by students, WP inadvertently (I assume) undermined the success already achieved by the mid-eighties in the use of both expressive and poetic writing in English classes. Personal-narrative, unfortunately, was not expressive in Britton's sense of the term, even though it was often presented as such. After all, it was inveterately a first-person narrative, with an actual, not a fantasized, "I" at the centre, telling about actual events to a familiar and nearby audience, all of which seem to fit the Britton definition. But, and it's a very big *but*, authentic expressive writing is by definition *non-revisable*. Its prototypal format is the friendly letter, written by an "I" to a familiar "you" and recounting events of mutual interest, often in ways that assume a shared context. The style is casual, associative, and cordial. No pen pal would write back and ask you to tidy up the coherence of paragraph two or flesh out your letter's description with more sprightly adjectives or suggest you get an editing partner to scrub up the punctuation. So, despite numerous superficial similarities, the kind of personal-narrative that dominates WP in elementary-school classrooms is not an expressive form: its successive drafting towards a perfected, publishable document does not replicate the one-off procedures of letter writing; and, more tellingly, the relationship of writer and reader in the expressive is diametrically opposite that in Writing Process.

But can we not say that such personal-narratives, because they *are* revised and polished up towards becoming a published story for anyone to read (the peer reviewers having faded discreetly away), ought to be classified as a type of poetic writing? Again the answer is no. While some pieces, by talented and persistent students, may survive the public drafting procedures of WP to become respectable first-person short stories (based on true events, as they say on TV), the near universal injunction of WP against in-role narrative or completely imagined or fantasized events, indicates at best a weak understanding of the projected, persona-driven shaping of the poetic mode and its "wild surmise" (to quote Keats again). Moreover, when WP theory disparages the use of powerful, initiating prompts; forbids the use of whole-class stimuli or preparatory sessions in favour of ten-minute mini-lessons; separates most writing from the contextual literature component;[6] and implies through its procedures that students first drafts of poems and stories are *invariably* weak or inchoate and therefore *always* in need of extensive and laboured revision, then there is no way it can be said that either the process or the product is poetic.[7]

In sum, the personal-narrative of WP is superficially expressive and superficially poetic, and lacks the vigour and uniqueness of either. In too many classrooms it has crowded out both poetic writing and useful expressive work in journals of various kinds. Its obsession with the workshop method (surely yet another manifestation of Dewey's progressivism) has made whole-class teaching *per se* suspect and has valorized student-selection of texts, with a corresponding decline in the core novel being taught to everyone by an expert teacher using a variety of appropriate methods. In its place we have workshop programmes characterized by the bifurcation of literature and composition, after nearly three decades of our trying to *integrate* them.

The Consequences of Theory

The attention paid to pedagogical theory waxes and wanes with time and circumstance, but misconceived theory always results in ineffective or muddled practice, even when teachers are unaware of its influence. The principles upon which teachers found their day-to-day teaching strategies have to pass two tests. First, they have to have been derived from a set of governing assumptions about the nature of what is taught (history, physics, geometry, the reading of literature, various modes of writing), which entails serious debate about the nature of being and knowledge. Few teachers have the time, inclination or need to participate in such arcane disquisition,[8] but their education *has* prepared them to handle theoretical questions on site and as they go, for they have at one time written history papers or poetry critiques, carried out lab experiments, and so on. Second, the expected results of teachers choosing a particular set of principled methods must be realized in practice: the predicted consequences must be seen and judged to be educationally worthwhile.

The case of Writing Process illustrates the validity of both these points. WP was never underpinned by any clear theory of how growth and maturation would occur over time. It ignored several decades of classroom success with competing methods that operated on opposite assumptions. And fifteen years of effort has failed to produce results in the classroom that are arguably superior to those achieved by other means that used one quarter of the time (less than that if integrative aspects are considered).[9] In brief, theory does matter, for thousands of misguided adherents to Writing Process sincerely believe that they are part of a methodological movement (and not merely purveyors of various tricks of method), a movement which they assume to have been founded upon irrefutable premises about how and why things work.

By the same token, the alternative teaching strategies for writing that I have outlined in chapter 4 must themselves continually be tested in theory and in practice. I have tried to show that the defining characteristics of the poetic and expressive modes of writing are based on reasonable assumptions, consistent with how and why poems, for example, get composed; how readers, both naive and mature, typically respond to them; how verse, fiction and expressive writing grow naturally out of early speech acquisition and preschool experience; how the hypothesis about the internalization of linguistic rules, structural grammars, and rhetorical moves — and their status as tacit knowledge and competency — is the most reliable one we have so far; and how growth in aesthetic reading most likely occurs over time in educationally nurturing classrooms.

It remains only to propose a theory of development for poetic writing: students learn to write over many years through (1) the imprinting of linguistic structures and values gained by repeated, qualitatively rich encounters with literary texts; (2) authentic composing activities where form and purpose combine to create crude, authentic, and successively advanced approximations, which are in turn treated as whole and complete by the teacher; and (3) the appropriation of models and criteria in a form which is increasingly explicit and more open to conscious manipulation.

The ability to write expressively grows as well but it appears to be a function more of general maturation in linguistic competency than a result of focussed learnings or deeply imprinted structures and moves. After all, the associative rhythm is meant to be free-flowing and more audience sensitive than it is rhetorically shaped or objective. Nonetheless, as Toby Fulwiler's inspiring collection of essays on the use of the journal from primary to graduate school illustrates,[10] the purpose and essential "I-you" posture of expressive writing remain undisturbed, while the diction and sentences reflect the educational level of the writer, the expectations of the privileged reader, and the formality of the subject matter.

In sum, a theory must provide practitioners with a plausible explanation of the "thing itself" and the mental processes it demands and engenders. Teaching strategies and curriculum decisions made in its name must be clear, workable, and general enough to be adapted effectively in the hubbub and joyful contingency of living classrooms. This latter point is critical, because no theory or set of pedagogical principles can be formulated in such a way as to yield teacher-proof methods guaranteed never to fail. Too many productive teaching methods have been jettisoned because they didn't work with 12G on the Friday before Thanksgiving! Sound theory ought to generate a range of suggestions for actual practice, and no more. For it is the individual English teacher who must choose the method, and then take responsibility for those moment-to-moment judgements without which any pedagogy, however dazzling, is merely technique. And that is as it should be.

Afterword

Implicit in the debates about the English curriculum since the 1950s have been the age-old dichotomies of the individual versus society, self-actualization versus socialization, freedom versus indoctrination, ethnic identity versus assimilation, special classes versus mainstreaming, and so on. Many of us can be forgiven for suspecting that the social side of these opposites usually means that middle-class values — however defined — will have been pre-selected narrowly from a wider, more polyglot and more generous range of norms, to be imposed upon every student. One size fits all. In general, I do not see any way in which a near universal, publicly funded educational system with a common curriculum of *some* kind can function otherwise. And "culture," whoever may be manipulating the levers that power it at any given moment — the bourgeoisie, the plutocracy, the proletariat (we can dream, can't we?) — is never fixed in time and space. It is as organic and protean and interactive as the poems, stories, songs, paintings and social mythology that embody and vivify it. And it is always in motion: a double movement, toing and froing among the generations. Although educators often *seem to be* drawing (or compelling) their charges into the frozen norms of the adult community — even as they mouth platitudes about developing critical thinkers and free spirits — the children themselves alter and recreate the culture as they move towards and into it. When exposed to poems, they will write poems; and no adult can predict what kind or how potent they might be, or what generative capacities may have been tacitly and permanently gained during the event. That is why the "paint-by-numbers" approach of Writing Process is so pernicious: it is an attempt by well-meaning adults to corral and legislate the child's poem-text, and, worse, to cut the child off from the wellspring of poetic language itself. In its place, of course, the child is offered a seemingly neutral set of composing protocols, into which and through which she is invited to pour content from her own personal experience, until it is revised and scrubbed up enough to be "published" and approved by her betters. The result is, inevitably, a narrowing and devaluing of the contradictory realities that characterize children's lives in the actual world.

For example, a working-class kid would be encouraged to write the first draft of a story (the personal-narrative) by drawing upon her own immediate experience — her home ground, as it were — and with the aid of her peer group (from her own social class and community) revise it until it was respectable enough to be pinned on the bulletin board for open house. Such procedures, repeated every day in thousands of North American schools, are not uneducational. Social skills are exercised and language learning does occur. Moreover, because the teacher is principally the manipulator of the protocols, the child's home experience and value system are, on the face of it, allowed unmediated expression. What's wrong with this picture? Beyond the problem of the values invisibly embedded in the protocols themselves and the ambiguity of the teacher's role (coach? sympathetic reader? collaborator? evaluator?), this working-class child has been denied the opportunity for any genuine transformation of either the initiating experience or the language made available to express it (impoverished and mundane as it is in this classroom). She will learn nothing fresh or unexpected or self-revelatory about her own life or the aesthetic means that might have illuminated it. As we have seen, merely expressing what you think and feel is not the same as projecting it into and through the transforming spectrum of poem or story.

In contrast to the restrictive and pseudo-personal method of Writing Process, the child here might have been immersed in psychologically powerful poems, stories and short films that depicted fresh aspects of her own experience of social class or startling insights into experience outside her own, texts whose content and metaphors she herself could draw upon (deliberately or unconsciously) to project her feelings and understandings into the self-revelatory words and objectifying form of a poem.

Just what sort of objectification or transformation are we talking about here? The latter term has a suspiciously apocalyptic ring to it. George Steiner describes it thus:

> As the act of the poet ... enters the precincts, spatial and temporal, mental and physical, of our being, it brings with it a radical calling towards change. The waking, the enrichment, the complication, the darkening, the unsettling of sensibility and understanding which follow on our experience of art are incipient with action ... Form is the root of performance. In a wholly fundamental, pragmatic sense, the poem, the statue, the

sonata are not so much read as they are *lived*. The encounter with the aesthetic is ... the most "ingressive," transformative summons available to human experiencing. Again, the shorthand image is that of an Annunciation, of "a terrible beauty" or gravity breaking into the small house of our cautionary being. If we have heard rightly the wing-beat and provocation of that visit, the house is no longer habitable in quite the same way as it was before. A mastering intrusion has shifted the light ...[1]

Are such claims not going too far? Are we not in danger of suggesting that an aesthetic component in the curriculum would revolutionize education, and society? Not quite. The transforming potential of the aesthetic is real enough, ever threatening to unsettle complacency. And while the literary arts as a result ought to be a significant, if controversial, part of the K-to-12 curriculum, they will not be the only elements of an English programme. The practical aspects of English will proceed apace, unperturbed: spelling, punctuation, grammar, usage, vocabulary expansion, media study, report writing, computer literacy, and so on. What Steiner has done for all of us in *Real Presences*, and I have attempted to do for education in this monograph, is to clear a space for the arts, a comfortable terrain where they can flourish and tempt us towards their "transformative summons."

What this means, in precise detail, for those children who are captive within their families, their neighbourhoods, their social class, their race or their gender is impossible to say. But what is certain is that any resistance to oppressive circumstance requires the deepest truths of our lives to be made plain to us. Aesthetic reading and poetic writing are paths to these truths, and to any legitimate resistance they engender.

Further, and finally, aesthetic reading and poetic writing in the curriculum should guarantee that the private self of each child — that secret and guarded home place inside each of us, which ought to be inviolable and indivisible — will be respected and invited to discover more about its being. In reality, we have two selves, a fact that has profound implications for teaching and learning, and which may at last help us see where some of the confusion lies in recent arguments about freedom and indoctrination. Paraphrasing Coleridge, William Walsh describes the two selves thus:

Coleridge describes what is ... a general characteristic of mankind, but one seen most clearly in the child. It is on one hand that restless search for release from the confinement of the single image of one self, and on the other a solicitude to keep the inviolable privacy of another self ... And by his distinction between the *representative* and the *real self*, between the image and the principle of individuality, Coleridge succeeds in easing the tension between the two terms of his paradox.[2] [Emphasis added]

The child in school, Coleridge implies, is a willing participant in those social and public aspects of the curriculum that assist in building up a representative image of the self within the community. Roles are taken up, tried on, and discarded or assimilated. In this regard, schools need to provide students with truly representative images from the surrounding culture, and, as far as possible, allow for the exercise of choice, of acceptance or rejection. In English this involves presenting students, as appropriate, with literary texts of psychological, sociological and aesthetic import, while permitting a reasonable choice of texts for independent reading and out-of-class projects. Walsh warns against doing otherwise:

For too many [teachers] maturity means a narrowing into a dull or resigned acceptance of a limited representative self and a disavowal or oblivion of the real self. Similarly, too much teaching offers insufficient opportunity and too feeble a provocation to enrich the image of self by imaginative participation in many modes of being; just as, all too frequently, it is, in the face of the helplessness of the child, an unjust invasion of the real self. But the mature adult — and this is what every teacher should be — is one who senses in others, because he has felt it in himself, beneath the image of the representative self the secret movements of a deeper self. For the image he has imaginative liberality, sympathy in feeling and tact in action; for the true self he has reverence.[3]

It is, then, the true self that is most likely to be nurtured — with courtesy, tact and respect — by apt engagement with aesthetic texts, along with the opportunity to compose authentic poems and stories. And, here, anything can happen because, whenever we read a poem or write a story, myth or fable, one inner voice is speaking freely and privately to another one: the poet to the reader, the writer to the writer. Here also the student is always on home ground, however uncongenial the schoolroom's space might be. Moreover, once an aesthetic experience is activated and given its own dedicated space, notions of gender, class, age, ability and ethnicity are, for the duration of the event at least, blissfully irrelevant. How long, how intense, or how transforming the consequent reverberations might be cannot be determined in advance. That is both the risk and the source of what is unique in aesthetic experience.

It is a risk worth taking.

Endnotes

Introduction

1. For an overview of some of these competing claims and their effect on one jurisdiction, see my historical account, *Stubborn Pilgrimage: Resistance and Transformation in Ontario English Teaching: 1960–1993* (Toronto: Our Schools/Our Selves Education Foundation, 1994), chs. 4–7.
2. John Dixon, for example, summarized the aims of the literature curriculum in the UK in *Education: 16–19: The Role of English and Communication* (London: Macmillan, 1979); for a discussion of these and their ubiquitousness in the English-speaking world, see my paper, "The View from Darien: The Drama of English in the High School Classroom," *The English Quarterly* 6, no. 1 (Spring 1982), 3–22.
3. The difficulty that North Americans began to have in the 1980s in finding a consensus on the appropriate goals for English is illustrated starkly in Kathryn MacIntosh, "The High School Literature Program: Book Selection, "'Censorship' and Dissenting Values" (PhD diss., University of Toronto, 1992). More than two dozen stakeholders are interviewed concerning what they consider to be the locus of authority (teacher, board, parents), apt teaching methods, and principles of text selection. Needless to say, there emerges no agreement, as special interest groups on the political left and right (and in the middle) offer contradictory agendas, and defend them with eloquence and vigour.
4. Excerpted from a speech given by Eco at York University in October, 1998, and printed in *The Globe and Mail*, 2 November 1998.
5. George Steiner, *Real Presences* (Chicago: University of Chicago Press, 1989), 1–2. Steiner concludes that those who believe in the coherence to be found in literature and other works of art — that is, their aesthetic way of effecting meaningfulness — are wasting their time in trying to out-argue positivists and deconstructionists or attempting to reconcile the opposing positions. An attempt at the latter is illustrated in recent books by two Canadian educators: Deanne Bogdan, *Re-Educating the Imagination: Toward a Poet-*

ics, Politics, and Pedagogy of Literary Engagement (Portsmouth, NH: Boynton/Cook/Heinemann, 1992) and Johan Aitken, *Masques of Morality: Women in Fiction* (Toronto: Women's Press, 1987). Both Aitken and Bogdan are painfully honest in their efforts to reconcile their deep love of literature as aesthetic with the pressing social concerns of feminism and the politics of equality. While they do not entirely succeed in convincing teachers that any such rapprochement is possible, they do leave us a vivid record of the endeavour and its schizoid difficulties.
6. Eco, *Ibid.*

Chapter 1

1. The reading-process models here have been derived from several sources: the work of Frank Smith in *Understanding Reading: A Psycholinguistic Analysis of Reading and Learning to Read* (New York: Holt, Rinehart and Winston, 1978); Don Holdaway's brilliant transformation of Smith's theories into pedagogically sound literacy programmes for primary school — particularly his insights into lap-reading and the use of cloze to demonstrate how prediction must operate as part of the cognition of comprehension — in *The Foundations of Literacy* (Sydney: Ashton-Scholastic, 1979); and Michael Polanyi's notion of focal and subsidiary factors in the reading of literature, which have been expanded upon in an excellent paper by Lloyd Brown, "Polanyi's Theory of Knowing," *Canadian Journal of English Language Arts* 2, no. 2 (1988), 5–19. See also, Michael Polanyi, *The Tacit Dimension* (Garden City, NY: Doubleday, 1966). The particular adaptations of the basic process to poetry and fiction are my own best guess at aspects of cognition we can never understand fully or prove.
2. For a detailed account of the role of prediction in reading, see Smith, *Understanding Reading*, 63–67. For a discussion of the phases of emergent literacy, see Holdaway, *The Foundations of Literacy*, 52–63, 88–102.
3. For a more detailed discussion of Smith's conception of comprehension, see my *Brave Season: Reading and the Language Arts in Grades Seven to Ten* (London, ON: The Althouse Press, 1983), 29–31. See also chapter 1 for a discussion of the developmental implications of the work of Smith and Holdaway, and a detailed developmental reading grid for grades four to nine.
4. Much of my understanding of the aesthetic in literature comes from my own experience as a poet and novelist and more than

thirty years as a teacher of literature and English methods, but the specific articulation of it owes much to the seminal writings of Susanne Langer: see *Feeling and Form* (New York: Scribner's, 1953); *Mind: An Essay on Human Feeling*, vol. 1 (Baltimore: Johns Hopkins Press, 1967), and *Philosophy in a New Key* (New York: Mentor, 1942).
5. Langer argues that music is the pre-eminent art form of pure connotation, and hence the most universal.
6. The necessity of closure in poetry, even in the most open-ended formats, is dramatically illustrated in children's attempts to find a rounding-off statement or device to close a thought or a rhetorical pattern set up previously in the text. See my research report, *The Dimension of Delight: A Study of Children's Verse Writing, Ages 11–13* (London, ON: The Althouse Press, 1988), 113–115 and appendix IV.

Chapter 2

1. For a detailed explanation of the three primary rhythms of human expression, see Northrop Frye, *The Well-Tempered Critic* (Bloomington: Indiana University Press, 1963), and my elaboration of them in *The Dimension of Delight*, 17–27.
2. See, for example, the lesson sequences in Don Holdaway, *Stability and Change in Literacy Learning* (London, ON: The Althouse Press, 1983), ch. 4.
3. This term is a useful generic one because it includes both spoken and written poetry. For a discussion of art-speech, see David Allen, *English Teaching Since 1965: How Much Growth?* (London: Heinemann, 1980), 101–103.
4. Of the numerous accounts of how poets go about their business and how they themselves view poetry, the most compelling for me is that of Archibald MacLeish, *Poetry and Experience* (Baltimore: Penguin, 1964). See, in particular, the discussion of sound values in poetry (in chapter 1).
5. Langer's explanation of presentational forms, denotation, connotation and virtuality is found in *Philosophy in a New Key*, but underpins all her later elaboration on the nature and effects of works of art. Her principal thesis — that human thought and its expression evolved from ritual and myth through poetic-presentational forms up to the discursive assertions of philosophy — permeates much mid-twentieth-century thinking in education and criticism.

6. For a discussion of the term "myth alive," see my paper, "Teaching the Canadian Mythology: A Poet's View," *Journal of Canadian Studies* 8, no. 1 (February 1973), 28–33. To observe the concept in action, see my paper on children's verse writing, "Myth Alive: Children's Poetry," *Classmate* 6, no. 1 (Fall 1975), 40–46.
7. For an interesting discussion of the relationship between the particular and the general in poetry, see William Walsh, *The Use of Imagination: Educational Thought and the Literary Mind* (London: Chatto and Windus, 1959), ch. 6.
8. For a snapshot of one contretemps involving the aesthetic and deconstructive "readings" of literature, see my paper, "The Search For Presence: A Reader-Response to Postmodern Literacy," *Our Schools/Our Selves* 6, no. 1 (September 1992), 90-110, and the papers that preceded and followed it: John Willinsky, "Postmodern Literacy: A Primer," *Our Schools/Our Selves* 3, no. 4 (June 1992); Willinsky, "An Authentic Pedagogy," *Our Schools/Our Selves* 6, no. 1 (September 1992), 110–114; and Jerome Meharchand, "*To Kill a Mockingbird* Revisited: A Response to the Gutteridge/Willinsky Debate," *Our Schools/Our Selves* 4, no. 2 (January-February 1993), 119–125. The postmodernist attacks on the apparent racism of *To Kill a Mockingbird* and the chauvinist piggery of Shakespeare's *Romeo and Juliet* are but two egregious examples of the confusion between the social analysis of text/subtext and the right of individuals, including students, to respond to these works as they were written and intended: aesthetically. It is the reader-viewer who makes the decision as to which glasses ought to be put on in any given situation.
9. For a summary of the question of reader's rights and a thought-provoking proposal on the matter, see Louise Rosenblatt, *The Reader; the Text; the Poem: A Transactional Theory of the Literary Work* (Carbondale IL: Southern Illinois University Press, 1978). Also helpful here is a collection of essays with a more radical perspective: Bill Corcoran and Emrys Evans, eds., *Readers, Texts, Teachers* (Upper Montclair NJ: Boynton/Cook, 1987).
10. See, for example, John Willinsky, *The New Literacy: Re-Defining Reading and Writing in Schools* (New York: Routledge, 1990) and, more briefly and iconoclastically, Pam Gilbert, "Post Reader-Response: the Deconstructive Critique," in Corcoran and Evans, *Readers, Texts, Teachers*.
11. Steiner, *Real Presences*, 152–165.

12. Paradoxically, while we must suspend our disbelief, we must at the same time pay passionate attention to the text and the business of re-enacting it. See Richard L. McGuire, *Passionate Attention: An Introduction to Literary Study* (New York: Norton, 1973).
13. See my earliest attempt to navigate these shoals: "The Affective Fallacy and the Student's Response to Poetry," *English Journal* 71, no. 2 (February 1972), 210–221. For a discussion of how consonance features assist poets in generating alternative words and meanings during the composing process, see my more recent paper, "The Coherence of Consonance in Poetry," *The English Quarterly* 16, no. 3 (Fall 1983), 3–10.
14. W.K. Wimsatt came closest to a reader-inclusive set of rules in "What to Say About a Poem" in W.K. Wimsatt, Josephine Miles and Laurence Perrine, *What to Say About a Poem and Other Essays* (Champaign, IL: NCTE, 1963). He too proposes a three-stage interpretive procedure; however, implicit in his method is the New Critical notion that there is a "best" reading (that is, an actual as opposed to an ideal one) if only we work diligently enough. The best illustration of the New Critical method in action is Cleanth Brooks and Robert Penn Warren, *Understanding Poetry* (New York: Holt, Rinehart and Winston, 1960). This book, aimed at the US college market, was a best-seller during the 1960s and 1970s.
15. See MacLeish, *Poetry and Experience*, 36–38 for an interesting discussion of a medieval ballad, "The Bailey Beareth the Bell Away," a poem that appears to be a straightforward description of events, but whose meaning deepens and intensifies when the spaces "between the lines" are filled in by the reader, and when allegorical intimations are given free rein. MacLeish demonstrates the power and influence of aesthetic anticipation, and shows that a tactful reading yields much without making the poem something more than it is.
16. See, for example, my paper, "The Hidden Meaning Syndrome," *The English Quarterly* 9, no. 1 and 2 (Spring/Summer 1976), 29–35. The charge of "reading into" is a serious one, and must be addressed if any sort of aesthetic-reading disposition is to be fostered in high-school students working with subtle, ambiguous poetry.
17. Martin Joos refers to literature as "frozen style"; that is, it is the "best butter" culled from the various registers of human speech

and frozen in a printed text. The notion of a frozen or fixed text is central to any discussion of the nature of poetry, for it raises the question of how and why it got frozen, and the corollary one: how and why we ought best to read it. Joos's little monograph is still an exemplary description of speech register. See Martin Joos, *The Five Clocks* (New York: Harcourt Brace, 1961).

18. Dylan Thomas is said to have rued the line "He ran his heedless ways" in what he otherwise considered a well-crafted poem (which had been revised some seventeen times).
19. Ambiguity may be discussed from many perspectives and in more minute detail. See, for example, William Empson, *Seven Types of Ambiguity* (London: Chatto and Windus, 1947).
20. For further discussion of the notion of student consent, see my *Brave Season*, 48–51.
21. While student selection of texts for independent reading has been vigorously promoted since the arrival of the paperback in schools thirty-five years ago, accompanied by Daniel Fader's messianic *Hooked on Books* (New York: Berkley, 1966), no one seriously suggested that students choose most or all of the books to be studied in class — that is, until the Whole Language approach became popular in elementary school during the 1980s and, with it, the imperatives of collaborative learning and the workshop methodology. The fallacy of students, particularly those in grades four to nine, choosing their own novels, for example, is cogently exposed in a paper by George Barker, "The Great Tradition: F.R. Leavis meets Judy Blume," *indirections* 15, no. 1 (March 1990). Barker distinguishes between those stories that confirm and those that stretch and challenge. For the most part, teachers will insist upon the latter.
22. Ian Underhill, my longtime colleague, who routinely astounded his students in the faculty of education by demonstrating the improbable but necessary connection between lesson planning and improvisation. For a glimpse into his pedagogy, see his section in my historical account, *Stubborn Pilgrimage*, 180–197. See also, Ian Underhill, *Family Portraits* (Toronto: McClelland and Stewart, 1978) and *Starting the Ark in the Dark: Teaching Canadian Literature in High School* (London, ON: The Althouse Press, 1977).
23. I tried this approach with a seminar group of gifted students in grade thirteen: each day for a week or so, one student chose a poem, had it duplicated, and brought copies to the group. The

other students and I then took a few minutes to read the poem, after which we began to talk informally about what we were getting from the poem. After they had made their most salient comments and we had heard from the student who chose the poem, I would then "talk out" my own running response — to demonstrate, tactfully, the range of interpretive moves available to a more experienced reader (and, incidentally, to let them know that I thus prepared every poem before bringing it into class: I was a reader as well as a teacher).
24. See my *Brave Season*, chs. 4 and 5. See also my earlier paper, "The Question of English: Toward a General Methodology," *The English Quarterly* 7, no. 2 (Summer 1974), 87–103. For a discussion of journal prompts, a form of question, and how to compose them, see my handbook, *Incredible Journeys: New Approaches to the Novel*, rev. ed. (London, ON: The Althouse Press), 14–16.
25. A glance or two at the teacher's guide for any of the major anthologies (or readers) of the 1970s and early 1980s will illustrate this point; for example, Holt Rinehart's *Impressions* or Ginn's *Starting Points*. "Content," "literal meaning," "inference," "personal response," "theme," and so on are used as if they were cognitively stable categories of comprehension, with no attempt to explain either their validity or their pedagogical usefulness in helping young readers to become increasingly competent by internalizing such categories. The real danger of inventing categories is illustrated in Leslie McLean's analysis of a province-wide reading test in Ontario, where he casts doubt upon the consistency, validity and usefulness of those time-honoured reading-comprehension categories, "main idea," "inference," "meaning from context" and "author's purpose." See Leslie McLean, *Report of the 1981 Field Trials in English and Mathematics: Intermediate Division* (Toronto: Ontario Ministry of Education, 1982), 10.
26. This is not to claim that students cannot make themselves into sophisticated readers of poetry and fiction by the time they are adult without being taught to do so in school. We have far too many extant examples that prove otherwise. But schools are charged with the responsibility of teaching as many students as possible to become proficient and engaged readers of literature. Autodidacts are few in number, though we might learn much about learning from them.

27. Response to literature is one of those catch-all expressions that is as vague and unhelpful as "Whole Language" or "student-centred learning." Influential books often cited as primers for this approach to teaching literature are David Bleich, *Readers and Feelings* (Urbana, IL: NCTE, 1975); Patrick Dias and Michael Hayhoe, *Developing Response to Poetry* (Milton Keynes, UK: Open University Press, 1988); and Robert Probst, *Response and Analysis: Teaching Literature in Junior and Senior High School* (Portsmouth, NH: Boynton/Cook, 1988). For a more empirical account of how students respond to literature, see Alan C. Purves and Richard Beach, *Literature and the Reader: Research in Response to Literature, Reading Interests, and the Teaching of Literature* (Urbana, IL: NCTE, 1972) and Jack Thomson, *Understanding Teenagers' Reading: Reading Processes and the Teaching of Literature* (Melbourne: Methuen; New York: Nichols Publishing, 1987).

28. For a discussion of some New Left pedagogy, see Willinsky, *The New Literacy*; Corcoran and Evans, *Readers, Texts, Teachers*; Stephen Zemelman and Harvey Daniels, *A Community of Writers* (Portsmouth, NH: Heinemann, 1988); and Brian Johnston and Stephen Dowdy, *Work Required: Teaching and Assessing in a Negotiated Curriculum* (Victoria, AUS: Martin Educational, 1988). The Whole Language/Writing Process obsession with student-initiated activities is demonstrated in the workshop approach in Nancie Atwell, *In the Middle: Writing, Reading and Learning With Adolescents* (Upper Montclair, NJ: Boynton/Cook, 1987). For a Canadian perspective, see Victor Froese, ed., *Whole Language: Practice and Theory* (Toronto: Allyn and Bacon, 1991). The best overview of the various voices on the left in the 1980s is Stephen Tchudi, ed., *Language, Schooling and Society*, Proceedings of the International Federation for the Teaching of English Seminar at Michigan State University, November 11–14, 1985 (Upper Montclair, NJ: Boynton/Cook, 1985).

29. Much of the Whole Language approach to teaching English is based on a vague Piagetian theory of learning, where the "environment" tempts students to learn something new whenever they decide they are interested and ready. The teacher can only enhance the possibilities of the environment, then watch and wait. The opposite theory, and the one underpinning everything in this book, is Vygotsky's concept of a zone of proximal learning,

wherein an adult or teacher places before the student a cognitive challenge that he or she is deemed ready to try; the teacher both pushes (by example and tactful challenging) and pulls (providing the necessary scaffolding, modelling and aptness of task). For Vygotsky's ideas on learning and teaching, see L.S. Vygotsky, *Thought and Language*, Eugenia Hanfmann and Gertrude Vakar, ed./trans. (Cambridge: M.I.T Press, 1962).

30. When the literal is ignored or skimmed, the result for student readers is usually a form of unrestrained allegorizing or free association. For a discussion, with examples, see my paper, "The Affective Fallacy and the Student's Response to Poetry."

31. The concept of fourth reading was suggested to me by my colleague, Ian Underhill.

32. For a discussion of aesthetic and efferent reading, see Rosenblatt, *The Reader, the Text, the Poem*, ch.3. Rosenblatt's laudable but somewhat tortuous attempt at sorting out the relative importance of the three stakeholders illustrates, for me, the futility of thinking too precisely on the event. Text, reader, and poem (the poet's and the reader's) are vital components, and teachers need to know that each has rights; but which component is apt to dominate at any given moment or in any given situation is a contingent matter, not to be spelled out absolutely or objectively. That is why teachers need to have clear principles and beliefs about poetry and teaching, and why teaching poetry is still an art.

33. For a detailed critique of this approach, see my *Stubborn Pilgrimage*, 168–174 and 247.

34. Jack Thomson argues for a carefully staged programme for teaching literature, reserving deconstructive analysis for the final stage: at the end of high school. See Thomson, *Understanding Teenagers' Reading*, 360–361.

35. For a look at the erosion of authority issue, see David Allen, *English Teaching Since 1965*. Allen traces the debate over "the disappearing dais" in the UK from the publication of John Dixon's influential post-Dartmouth monograph *Growth Through English* (Oxford: Oxford University Press, 1967/1976) to 1980, where Dixon's fuzzy "activities" methodology was suddenly buttressed and merged with the North American workshop methodology of Whole Language and Writing Process. The teacher's role as authority and what that has meant since 1960 is discussed throughout my *Stubborn Pilgrimage*. For a contemporary critique of Dixon's activities model, see my paper, "The Subject-

Centred Curriculum: Last Chance or Lost Cause?" *The English Quarterly* 4, no. 4 (Winter 1971), 18–26.

36. Again, the term "independent study" is a vague, catch-all concept that appears to refer to just about any work done by a student that is not explicitly supervised by the teacher. The consequences of such vagueness were evident in Ontario post-1984, when an independent study component was made mandatory in senior high school, but not defined. See Donna Hammond, "Approaches to the Independent Study Unit in the English OAC 1 Course" (MEd, University of Western Ontario, 1989).
37. For an excellent discussion of fairy tales in the curriculum, in the context of both feminist and aesthetic concerns, see Johan Aitken, "Myth, Legend and Fairy Tale: 'Serious Statements about our Existence,'" in *Growing With Books*, Book 1 (Toronto: Ontario Ministry of Education, 1988) and Cornelia Hoogland, "Poetics, Politics and Pedagogy of Grimm's Fairy Tales" (PhD diss., Simon Fraser University 1993).
38. See, once again, John Harker's paper, "The Great Tradition Revisited."
39. For a review of the *sturm und drang* over the growth-through-English pedagogy of the late sixties and early seventies, see my *Stubborn Pilgrimage*, ch. 4 and Allen's *English Teaching Since 1965/6*.
40. The charges of racism are particularly serious when they are brought against anti-racist classics like *Huckleberry Finn* and *To Kill a Mockingbird*. For an excellent discussion of this issue, see William Hare, *What Makes a Good Teacher* (London, ON: The Althouse Press, 1993), ch. 4. For an historical overview of literary censorship, see Kathryn MacIntosh, "The High School Literature Program," ch. 1.
41. For a detailed discussion of the text-selection process, including a specific set of criteria for grades seven to twelve, see my two-part paper, "Truth and Consequences: Selecting Literature for Grades 7–12/OAC," *indirections* 17, no. 1 and 17, no. 2 (March 1992 and June 1992), 32–41 and 38–48.
42. For a discussion of tact and its essential role in teaching, see Max van Manen, *The Tact of Teaching: The Meaning of Pedagogical Thoughtfulness* (London, ON: The Althouse Press, and New York: SUNY Press, 1991).
43. These two terms are discussed in Kieran Egan, *Educational Development* (New York: Oxford University Press, 1979),

99–102. Egan also introduces a third kind of learning on these pages: entertainment. For a discussion of the way primary-school children "think mythically," see Egan, *Teaching as Story Telling* (London, ON: The Althouse Press, 1986) and the more theoretical account in *Primary Understanding: Education in Early Childhood* (New York and London: Routledge, 1988).

44. Holdaway, *The Foundations of Literacy*. The critical concept of automaticity, a form of tacit processing, is discussed on pages 171–180.
45. Ken Goodman, *What's Whole in Whole Language?* (Richmond Hill, ON: Scholastic, 1986). The functions of written language are listed on page 23. For a description of a typical Whole Language classroom, see pages 38–42. One of the great disservices Whole Language has done is to forever confuse teachers about the meaning of the term "whole." Holdaway succeeded in convincing the profession that "holistic" learning was natural among children, and carefully laid out the cognitive framework within which it operated. For him, and me, it meant the kind of "all-at-once" grasp of meaning associated with our reading of aesthetic texts, as well as those sudden, creative bursts of role play and mimicry, where automatic competencies come fully into play. Goodman and others have managed to hijack the term and apply it to a series of vaguely-defined phenomena having to do with what is real and consciously purposeful, and, sometimes, merely with whatever is opposed to rote phonics instruction.
46. This often-observed, somewhat contradictory reaction of children to reading and writing rhymed verse is confirmed in a US study by Ann Terry: *Children's Poetry Preferences: A National Survey of Upper Elementary Grades* (Urbana, IL: NCTE, 1974).
47. The nature and purpose of the literature journal (a type of response journal) is explained in my handbook, *Incredible Journeys*, 10–12. A framework for evaluation is given on page 13.
48. For a description of this jotting technique, see my research report, *The Dimension of Delight*, ch. 1.
49. For a perceptive analysis of the middle-school student and the traits that mark this "romantic" stage of learning, see Kieran Egan, *Imagination in Teaching and Learning* (London, ON: The Althouse Press, 1992). Egan's complete four-stage developmental model of learning was first proposed in his *Educational Development* (New York: Oxford University Press, 1979).

50. See Nancie Atwell, *In the Middle*. Some aspects of my somewhat harsh critique of this book and the curriculum approach it has spawned can be better understood from the perspective of my analysis of Writing Process, whose even more muddled assumptions Atwell accepts uncritically. See chapter 5 of this monograph for further discussion of the Writing Process movement.
51. A useful taxonomy of reader-types and fiction-reading stages for the middle years appears in *Incredible Journeys* (rev. ed.), 76–79. In brief, stage one readers are print-shy, stage two readers prefer basic narratives, stage three readers are enriched-story readers, and stage four readers are autonomous readers and often gifted students. I use these descriptive terms throughout the rest of the book. For a more detailed discussion of autonomous readers, see my paper, "Teaching Literature for Cognitive Development: A Double Perspective," *indirections* 6, no. 3 (Fall 1981), 28–40. In the latter, I introduce two useful descriptive terms: contextual and autonomous readers.
52. For a more nuanced version of this lesson, see my paper, "Sound and Sense in the Teaching of Poetry," *The English Quarterly* VI, 3 (Fall 1973), 239-248.
53. "in Just-". Copyright 1923, 1951, © 1991 by the Trustees for the E. E. Cummings Trust. Copyright © 1976 by George James Firmage, from COMPLETE POEMS: 1904–1962 by E. E. Cummings, edited by George J. Firmage. Used by permission of Liveright Publishing Corporation.

Chapter 3

1. The imperative for closure in composing a poem is convincingly illustrated, though unexplainable, in the hundreds of student poems that appear in my *Dimension of Delight*. See, in particular, appendix IV. The compulsion to close or round off a poem in some way appropriate to whatever pattern has been set up (the variety of such efforts demonstrated in appendix IV is amazing, considering how few standard, rhymed formats are used by the students) strongly supports the notion that young children have a developed sense of text, even beyond their more obvious grasp of story-grammar.
2. Once again I am indebted to Northrop Frye for this account of prose rhythm. See Frye, *The Well-Tempered Critic*, ch 1. Frye also points out that each of the rhythms has its "pseudo" versions (pp. 36–38), and these make illuminating reading for English teachers.

3. For a lively account of the casual and consultative registers, see Joos, *The Five Clocks*.
4. For a discussion of how children learn about syntax and story-grammar during lap reading, see Holdaway, *The Foundations of Literacy*, ch. 3. For a brief introduction to the general acquisition of language by children, see Peter A. and Jill G. de Villiers, *Early Language* (Cambridge: Harvard University Press, 1979). For a discussion of children's early attraction to story or tale, see André Favat, *Child and Tale* (Urbana, IL: NCTE, 1977) and Arthur N. Applebee, *The Child's Concept of Story: Ages Two to Seventeen* (Chicago: University of Chicago Press, 1978).
5. See Egan, *Teaching as Story Telling* and his background theory book, *Primary Understanding* for an account of the pedagogical implications of story form.
6. The importance of books, and of novels in particular, is eloquently testified to in Joseph Gold, *Read For Your Life: Literature as a Life-Support System* (Toronto: Fitzhenry and Whiteside, 1990) and G. Robert Carlsen and Anne Sherrill, *Voices of Readers: How We Come to Love Books* (Urbana, IL: NCTE, 1988).
7. For a more detailed discussion of the cognitive-processing aspects of reading (and teaching) literature, see my paper, "Literature and Reading in High School: The Cognitive Dimensions," *indirections* 7, no. 2 (Spring 1982), 27–38. See also *Brave Season*, ch. 4.
8. Students in grades four to nine prefer to read novels on their own, but enjoy reading and discussing short stories in class or in their discussion groups. As to why this should be so, we can only speculate. The kind of novel preferred is the first-person romance — hero-centred, action-packed, and exotic. Egan's taxonomy of the romantic qualities of students in these grades helps to explain why. See his *Romantic Understanding: The Development of Rationality and Imagination, Ages 8–15* (New York and London: Routledge, 1990). See also my paper, "The Romance Novel in the Intermediate Grades," *indirections* 3, nos. 3/4 (Spring/Summer 1978), 37–42.
9. Anne Gutteridge, a tutor of primary reading whom I have had the privilege of observing on a number of occasions, has helped beginners who have suffered too much instruction (and collapsed among the detritus of rules) or not enough instruction (that is, letter-sound correspondences — phonics — were not taught or demonstrated, and hence print remained a maze of twisted serifs). The either-or brouhaha over phonics that has raged and outraged for the past fifteen years is, alas, based on a false dichotomy. The

question has always been *how* to teach sound-letter correspondence and morphology so that they support and catalyze emergent reading, as Holdaway has maintained and demonstrated; see his *Foundations of Literacy*, 81–103.
10. The results of an overly enthusiastic "prep" by the teacher are usually disastrous, especially if biographical information is provided in advance and out of context. Telling a grade-eleven class that some feminists consider Shakespeare to have been a misogynist, just before they are to view a film or listen to a recording of *Romeo and Juliet*, is not likely to enhance an untrammelled aesthetic response or promote the dramatic manifestation of issues and themes.
11. Again, see Egan, *Romantic Understanding* and *Imagination in Teaching and Learning*.
12. For an egregious example of reading by doing, see Michael Hayhoe and Stephen Parker, *Working With Fiction* (London: Edward Arnold, 1984), *passim*. See also Michael Benton and Geoff Fox, *Teaching Literature: Nine to Fourteen* (Oxford: Oxford University Press, 1985). Benton and Fox replicate the methodology and the fallacy, despite the fact that they try hard to maintain an aesthetic dimension on first reading and use the response journal as a major device. But they confuse second reading and third-reading activities in such a way that their students will still see rereading as a *doing* phenomenon, not a meditative, mental activity. Further examples may be found in a popular Shakespeare series where, after each scene and every act, students are obliged to perform detailed and often complex extension activities — writing letters in role, debating an issue raised *in situ* and often incidentally, rewriting a scene in modern idiom — before the whole play has been read and discussed. See *HBJ Shakespeare Series* (Toronto: Harcourt, Brace, Jovanovich, 1988–90).
13. The story has been excerpted from Farley Mowat's *The Curse of the Viking Grave*, chs. 19 and 20, and may be found in the anthology *Journeys I*, Jim French, comp. (Toronto: McClelland and Stewart, 1979), 27–42.
14. The four stages of reading fiction are described in detail in my *Incredible Journeys*, rev. ed., 75–79.

Chapter 4

1. The bible of the movement was Marjorie L. Hourd's *The Education of the Poetic Spirit* (London: Heinemann, 1949). Other influ-

ential books were David Holbrook, *The Secret Places* (London: Methuen, 1964), and Kenneth Koch, *Wishes, Lies and Dreams* (New York: Chelsea House, 1970).
2. Several good examples of this 1960s pedagogy in creative writing may be found in *Rhetoric: A Unified Approach to English Curricula* (Toronto: OISE Press, 1970). See in particular the elementary-school section (pp. 21–63).
3. Dozens of collections of student verse were published during the decade, the most striking of which is *Miracles: Poems by Children of the English-Speaking World*, Richard Lewis, ed. (New York: Simon and Schuster, 1966).
4. James Britton, Tony Burgess, Nancy Martin, Alex McLeod and Harold Rosen, *The Development of Writing Abilities (11–18)* (London: Macmillan, 1975).
5. See Britton et al., *Writing Abilities (11–18)*, 88–90. The summary here is my own extrapolation from Britton's work. For an analysis of some of the conceptual confusions in Britton's categories and his claims for their developmental potential, see my paper, "Writing Process: Alarums and Confusions; Part One: Prelude to Process: The Britton Hypotheses," *indirections* 15, no. 3 (September 1990), 65–78. Further comments appear in the endnotes of my *Dimension of Delight*, 131–133, 134–135, 140.
6. Jason's poem and the miracle of children's verse are discussed in detail in my paper, "Myth Alive: Children's Poetry." See also, Robert Druce, *The Eye of Innocence: Children and Their Poetry* (Leicester: Brockhampton Press, 1965) and Jack Beckett, *The Keen Edge: An Analysis of Poems by Adolescents* (London: Blackie and Sons, 1965).
7. Curiously enough, though Britton is responsible for defining and legitimating expressive writing in the curriculum, the journal in its many guises has become the principal expressive format in North American schools, while in the UK the talk-to-writing aspect of the expressive has led to a near deification of group talk and its consequences. For an overview of the uses of the journal from kindergarten to graduate school, see Toby Fulwiler, *The Journal Book* (Upper Montclair, NJ: Boynton/Cook, 1987).
8. For a more detailed account of HSQR, see my *Dimension of Delight*, ch. 1.
9. Excerpted from Wendy Jackson, *Study-Guide on The Secret Garden* (London, ON: The Althouse Press, 1992), 8–9.

10. Excerpted from Mark Dutton, *Study-Guide on Huckleberry Finn* (London, ON: The Althouse Press, 1992) 10–11.

Chapter 5

1. See, for example, Alan Coman, *The Uses of Film in the Teaching of English* (Toronto: OISE Press, 1971).
2. For an account of how Gravesian writing-process methods affected English teaching, see *Stubborn Pilgrimage*, ch. 7.
3. See my paper, "Writing Process: Alarums and Confusions; Part Two: Grave Doings: The New Orthodoxy," *indirections* 15, no. 4 (December 1990), 1–18.
4. The approval rating for Writing Process varies across the K-to-12 spectrum: the lower the grade, the more highly teachers speak of WP. For this information and a comprehensive report card on Writing Process, see Sarah Freedman, *Reponses to Student Writing*, NCTE Research Report No. 23 (Urbana, IL: NCTE, 1987). Freedman also comments on the middle-class orientation of WP, a factor that calls into question the general applicability of WP to the wider school population. See Freedman's "Summary of Findings" for these and other relevant criticisms.
5. See Lucy M. Calkins, *The Art of Teaching Writing* (Portsmouth, NH: Heinemann, 1986), 317–321. For further discussion of this issue and Calkins' admission, see *The Dimension of Delight*, 137–138 (endnote 18).
6. One of the more influential books in promoting and disseminating Writing Process and the workshop method is Atwell's *In the Middle*. Tellingly, the book is comprised of two separate and discrete halves, one devoted to reading, the other to writing. Writing workshops and associated mini-lessons are carried out in one hour of the day and reading workshops in another. Any crossover of skills, motivation and learnings is either coincidental or anecdotal. For instance, no sustained effort is made to carry ideas, themes or discussions from the reading programme into the writing one — where, alas, the ubiquitous personal-narrative reigns unchallenged. Also, in the reading workshops, there is no immediate response to literature in journals, only conversations about books between teacher and (mostly) individual students. In short, the manifold uses of the expressive have barely been tapped in Atwell's curriculum, and any aesthetic excitement that might be raised in reading class will have to cool its heels until writing class later in the day or week.

7. The labyrinthine confusions of the process-product debate would stun a minotaur. When "process" can mean anything from keeping a tidy log (numbered and dated) of your successive drafts to the manifestation of deeply internalized cognitive "moves," the debate itself is rendered meaningless. The potential long-term harm of valorizing process is that the critical concept of progressive approximation is lost or trivialized. Student products are *always* approximations of a sort, even when they are aesthetically and emotionally dazzling.
8. Robin Barrow argues his way towards this extreme and hapless position — where teachers, in order to be considered autonomous professionals, must make themselves into philosopher kings. See, *Giving Teaching Back to Teachers* (London, ON: The Althouse Press, 1984), 268–269.
9. Integrated approaches to teaching English had a proven track record long before Graves's Writing Process, Atwell's reading workshop, and Goodman's Whole Language usurped centre stage in the 1980s, as even a glance at the resource sections of chapters 2, 3 and 4 will confirm. The popularity and success of James Moffett's *A Student-Centered Language Arts Curriculum, Grades K-13* (Boston: Houghton-Mifflin, 1973) with its many kits and class sets of novels, and its elaborated theory in Moffett's *Teaching the Universe of Discourse* (Boston: Houghton-Mifflin, 1968), surely deserved the critical attention of anyone setting out a new and contrary prospectus for teaching English. Moreover, the consensus around the efficacy of the integrated language arts approach in the early eighties is evident in Beverly Busching and Judith Schwartz, eds., *Integrating the Language Arts in the Elementary School* (Urbana, IL: NCTE, 1983). But I can find no evidence of the collaborative-workshop methodology being *argued* in the context of these previous, proven approaches, except to set up straw dogs and dismiss them in a cursory paragraph or two. See, for example, Atwell, *In the Middle*, 18–19 and Goodman, *What's Whole in Whole Language?*, 7–8.
10. Fulwiler, *The Journal Book*.

Afterword

1. Steiner, *Real Presences*, 143.
2. Walsh, *The Use of Imagination*, 15.
3. *Ibid.*, 15–16.

Index

advance preparation, 81
aesthetic reading: and development of literacy, 46; fourth encounter, 43-44; growth in, 82; initial encounter, 35, 40, 52, 53, 59-60; and meaning, 25-29; pedagogical principles, 34-45; place in English programmes, 46; process, 11-19; reader's age level, 35-37; role of teacher in, 34-35; second encounter, 38, 40, 53, 54, 60-61; third encounter, 40, 41-42, 60
aesthetic transposition, 42
aliment, 49
alliteration, 18
ambiguity, 29, 31-33, 48, 59, 71
anthologies, 57
anticipation and confirmation, 77
anxiety and relief, 77
arrangement, 76
art-speech. *See* poetry
associative meaning, 15, 23, 32, 65, 105
associative reflection, 80
Atwell, Nancie, 58

Beckett, Jack, 113
Blake, William, 30
Britton, James, 72, 101-2
"Burnt Norton," 23

cadence line, 21
Calkins, Lucy, 116, 117, 118
Cameron, Jack, 113
choral reading, 55
chunking, 8, 80
class, 122-23
Cleator, Pat, 97
closure: aesthetic, 15, 40; sense of, 10, 11
Coleridge, Samuel Taylor, 24, 124-25
connotative meaning. *See* associative meaning
crafting, 74-75
Cramer, Ronald L., 113
creative writing movement, 101, 115
culture, 122
Cummings, E.E., 61, 62

Deimling, Carol Keyes, 98
denotation, 15, 21
Dewey, John, 119
disbelief, suspension of, 25-26, 27-29, 34, 70-71
discussion, classroom, 55-57, 60, 106
dramatic pauses, 74
Druce, Bruce, 113

editing. *See* skimming/editing
Egan, Kieran, 49, 54
Eggins, Geoffrey, 98
Eliot, T.S., 23
empathy, 77, 79

English programmes: kindergarten to grade three, 49-51; grades four to nine, 51-58; grades ten to twelve, 58-67; debates about curriculum, 122; organization of units, 60; place of aesthetic reading in, 46; student-selected texts, 46-47; study of literature, 48-49
Esbensen, Barbara Juster, 113
experience, real-life, 90
expressive writing, 53-54, 101-6
extension, 58, 61, 87, 88, 95-96

feeling-thought, 14, 24, 42, 47, 48, 103
fiction: aesthetic meaning in, 76; aesthetic qualities, 70-77; appropriate selection of, 84-85; basic-narrative readers, 77-78, 80, 84, 85; differences between story and poem, 71-72; enriched readers of story-text, 78-79, 80, 85; story, 74-75; structure in, 72; surface text, 77-78; teaching, 83-96; tone in, 75
figures of speech. *See* metaphor
first drafts, 107, 108-9
first-person narrative, 73-74
first-person persona, 103-4
first reading: fiction, 83-84, 92-93, 115; poems, 35, 40, 52, 53, 59-60
focal-peripheral switching, 77-78, 80
fourth-reading activities, 43-44
French, Jim, 97, 98
'from-to' processing, 9
Frye, Northrop, 21, 72

Geller, Linda Gibson, 67
gestalt insight, 15
Gillanders, Carol, 67
Goodman, Ken, 51
Graves, Donald, 116, 117, 118
Gutteridge, Don, 68, 97, 98, 100, 113

Hayhoe, Michael, 68
high stimulus/quick response procedures, 108-10
"Highwayman, The," 32
Holbrook, David, 113
Holdaway, Don, 8, 50, 68
holding-in-abeyance. *See* tolerance/holding-in-abeyance
Hoogland, Cornelia, 98
Hourd, Marjorie, 114

ideology, 47-48, 76
imagery, 22
images, 15, 18, 125
immersion, in aesthetic text, 49-50
independent study, 44, 45-46
inert learning, 49
inference, 78
internalization, 117
interpretation, 29-34, 37, 59-60, 71
intertextuality, 44
introduction, 85

Jackson, David, 99
jingles, 21
journal: expressive, 105, 106, 115; student-response, 53-54, 55, 107

Keats, John, 28
Kirby, Dan, 114
Koch, Kenneth, 114

Langer, Susanne, 10, 13, 23
language: acquisition of, 21; rightness of, 77 language acquisition, preschool, 50
letter, friendly, 109, 119
Liner, Tom, 114
literacy, development of, 46
literature: classic, 49; ideology in, 47-48

McRoberts, Eleanor, 97
Malloch, Jean and Ian, 99
meaning: ambiguity in, 29, 31-33; associative, 15, 23, 32; in fiction, 76, 87; in narrative-expository works, 8-11; in poems, 22, 25-26; precise, 31; in prose discourse, 22
metacognition, 116-17
metaphor, 29-33, 52, 64, 65
metrics, 13, 22, 23-24
mimicked voices, 74
mood. *See* tone
Moss, Joy F., 99
motives, 86-87
Mowat, Farley, 90-96
music: associative meanings in, 23; and verse, 21
"My Last Duchess," 38-39
mystery, 81
myths, 76

narrative, 73-74, 75, 77
New Criticism, 28, 38
non-analytic ways of teaching poetry, 55-57
noticed moments, 15
novels: core, 85; historical, 90; straight-ahead, 77
Noyes, Alfred, 32
nursery rhymes, 21

"On First Looking into Chapman's Homer," 28

Parker, Stephen, 68
part-whole phenomenon, 25-28
patterns, 64
pedagogical theory and practice, 120-21
personal-narrative, 118-20
Plattor, Emma, 113
plot, 82
poems: aesthetic makeup of, 20-29, 39; comparison of, 41-42; composition, 24-25; effect on mature readers, 40-41; lyric, 13-19, 20-29; meaning in, 22, 25-26; for middle-school years, 55; as non-discursive representational forms, 22-23, 39; and thought, 14, 23-24
poetic writing, 105-7, 108-13; revision in, 116-17; theory of development, 121
poetry: classic, 49, 58; closed-form, 107; emotional impact in, 22-23; modern, 39; non-aesthetic reading of, 42-43; open-form, 107; rhymed, 51-52; student, 59; teaching of, 21-22; writer-reader relationship, 25-26, 33-34
point of view, 75; transposed, 109
Polanyi, Michael, 8
political correctness, 48
prediction, 8, 79, 81
preschoolers, 72-73
presentation, student, 55-56
Probhst, Robert, 68
productive pauses, 78, 79
progressivism, 119
projection, 30-31, 102-3

propaganda, 47-48
prose: discourse, 22; discursive, 22-23; rhythm, 20, 21, 72-73
Protherough, Robert, 99

questions, teacher-initiated, 37, 38-39

read-alouds, 84, 86, 91, 92
reader-centred movement, 38
reading: choral, 55; efferent, 76; fiction, 77-82; independent, 50; informal, 56-57; narrative-expository text, 8-10; reflective, 52; story-line reflection, 79-80, *See also* aesthetic reading
reflective pause, 11, 79
reflective scan, 81
repetition, sounds, 22
revision, 116-17
rhythm, 13, 22, 25, 28, 75; associative, 20, 72, 105; prose, 20, 21, 72-73; verse, 20-21
Rosenblatt, Louise, 42

second reading: fiction, 86-87, 93-94;
poems, 38, 40, 53, 54, 60-61
self, private, 124-26
sentence, 21, 72
sequence of events, 74
shaping, 74-75
Shelley, Percy Bysshe, 24
skimming/editing, 80
Smith, Frank, 8
social context, 44
sociological analysis. *See* thematic analysis
Socratic method, 38
Somers, Albert, 99

speech-phrase, 72
Steiner, George, 19, 25, 26, 47, 118, 123, 124
story, 74-75; virtual, 70, 77, 83-84, 86, 90
story-grammar, 72-73, 75, 83
story-line reflection, 79-80
story-rhetoric, 77-78
story-thought, 70
student-response: discussions, 42, 60; journal, 53-54, 55, 107
subvocalization, 14, 17-18
surface features, 8, 12, 14, 17
surprise, 77
suspense, 77, 81
symbol, 64, 82
symmetry of event, 77

teacher-directed approach, 46-47
teachers: intervention, 37-39, 47; pedagogical role of, 34-45; selection of text, 36-37, 47; understanding of aesthetic reading, 34-35; and working-class students, 123
thematic analysis, 44, 45-46, 61
third reading: extension, 89, 95-96; fiction, 88-89, 94-95; poems, 40, 41-42, 60, 61
Thompson, Denys, 114
timbre, 75
tolerance/holding-in-abeyance, 81
tone, 63, 64, 65, 66, 74, 75
transactional writing, 101
transformation, 123-24
transposition, 50; aesthetic, 42

Underhill, Ian, 100

values, 76, 123

verse: adjuncts of, 22; expressed form, 20; mnemonic value of, 20-21
Vygotsky's zone of proximal learning, 54, 134-35n.29

Walsh, William, 124-25
Whole language approach, 38
"Word, The," 16-18, 27
workshop method, 119-20
Worthington, Janet, 99
writing, poetic, 57-58
Writing Process method: advocates, 38; critiqued, 117-20, 122-23; procedural process, 117; theory of, 116

zone of tacit awareness, 9, 13, 78